The Oracle's Golden Step

The Curious Travels of a Truck Driving Soothsayer

Brian R Bussard

The Oracle's Golden Step
by Brian R Bussard

ISBN :   978-0-9769678-3-5 (softcover edition)

The fictional characters in this book are trained stunt professionals. Do not attempt this at home.

Publisher's Cataloging-in-Publication Data
Names: Bussard, Brian R., author.
Title: The Oracle's golden step : the curious travels of a truck driving soothsayer / Brian R. Bussard.
Description: Lasal, UT: Hobbs Media, LLC, 2023.
Identifiers: LCCN: 2023945847 | ISBN: 978-0-9769678-4-2(hardcover) | 978-0-9769678-6-6 (paperback) | 978-0-9769678-5-9 (ebook)
Subjects: LCSH Success in business. | Success. | Entrepreneurship. | New business enterprises. | Finance, personal. | BISAC BUSINESS & ECONOMICS / General | BUSINESS & ECONOMICS / Decision-Making & Problem Solving | BUSINESS & ECONOMICS / Entrepreneurship | BUSINESS & ECONOMICS / Finance / Wealth Management | BUSINESS & ECONOMICS / Motivational | BUSINESS & ECONOMICS / New Business Enterprises | SELF-HELP / Personal Growth / Success
Classification: LCC HD62.5 .B87 2023 | DDC 658.1/1--dc23

Chapter One

What if I fail to convince him? What if he says no? Or worse, what if he says yes? Am I prepared for this?

"I'm not a…" I glanced around to see if anyone was within earshot.

After all, it is normal for young adults my age to move back in with their parents after college. It is normal to stay for a few years. It is normal to stay in their basement, however, this is not my case. My bedroom door is right next to my parents.

It is even normal that their wallpaper is the same dinosaur print their father hung up over two decades ago. It is normal to be hitting the snooze button on the same alarm clock they had in seventh grade, although there's no reason to set it. There is no place that I need to be.

Standing in the parking lot of the truck stop near the outskirts of town, I picked up my duffel bag. Not owning a decent set of luggage and having to use the same bag I used to carry my gym clothes in was also normal for my age.

The asphalt had many cracks in it. In this town, the only spot which had a smooth lot was the church. Being the only place to ride a skateboard in this town, you would catch only the children riding one. The teenagers found it conflicting.

None of that mattered, though. I was not a skater. I was not anything. I was not anyone.

*

"Are you the Oracle?" I asked the man who was sitting alone at the restaurant which was built into the truck stop.

He appeared to be in his late forties with long brown hair and a beard, both just starting to show some pepper white, and had weathered green tattoos covering his right arm and partway up his neck. He wore a plaid button-up shirt with cutoff sleeves that was omitting a small odor.

When I walked through the doors of the station, I noticed the usual items—candy bars, CB radios, and a whole counter full of coffee pots and such. What really caught my eye was that they still sold old cassette tapes.

I could describe the restaurant section as being frozen in time, of which was 1972. Everything was dark brown, artificial wood and orange laminate.

The cash register counter was so worn that it hardly had a sharp edge left on it. The multicolored patterned carpet was turning back into a single color and duct tape held some spots down at the seams.

Every table had an ashtray even though they didn't allow smoking. They wanted everyone to understand that they still welcomed smokers—just don't smoke.

"Who wants to know?" he grumbled, though not losing focus on his fresh bowl of breakfast chili.

"Snow Queen Sally told me I could find you here."

"Snow Queen Sally?" He finally looked up at me.

"Yes, may I have a seat?"

"In Mexico, it is a tradition that if there is an empty seat at your table, strangers are welcome. I figured you should know that in case you ever find yourself there, so you won't be shocked."

I went to drop my gym bag on the carpet, then hesitated and threw it on the bench seat across from him. I followed it and grabbed a menu to glance at—although I wasn't planning on ordering anything. "Thanks for giving me a moment of your time."

"How do you know Snow Queen Sally?" he asked.

"You could say that she's a friend of a friend, I guess. How is it you know her?"

"Friend of a friend." He went back to his chili.

"She said you are the person to come to for answers. That's why they call you the Oracle."

"I've been called worse. My friends call me Jimmy Z."

"Pleasure to meet you, Jimmy Z."

"It's Oracle to you," he said making it clear that we were not friends.

"Sorry—Oracle. Are you the one who can help me?"

"What answers are you looking for?"

"I graduated college a while ago with a major in commerce and finance. She said that you could explain to me what they don't write in the books."

I won't bother to mention what I have been doing in these empty years since graduating. I want him to think that I still have hope.

"Hmm… Suppose I'm the right man for that."

"Then do you care if I tag along for a bit on your deliveries?"

"I reckon any friend of a friend of Snow Queen Sally's is a friend of a friend of mine."

"May I call you Jimmy Z then?"

"No."

*

"Are you settled in?" he asked.

Since the cab of the semi-truck, or eighteen-wheeler as they called it, had virtually no room, I had to place my tiny duffel bag on the floor and rest my feet on it.

I'm not familiar enough with them to explain it extensively, however, these few things are what I can mention about it. It was silver with *The Beast* painted in black lettering on the front bumper. It was a cab-over style, which meant there was no hood. Past the windshield was nothing but a sharp drop off and open-air.

There was no sleeper cab, thus no living quarters. The cab ended right behind our seats. They call these day cabs because they are primarily used for single day trips. That was okay with me because it meant I would be home every night. Since I already packed my bag, I thought I might as well bring it with me.

The last thing to be said about it is that it was ancient. Possibly even older than power steering, as indicative of the size of his arms. If it came with it originally, then the power part of it must have gone out long ago.

The trailer was a 48-foot box unit with a refrigerant reefer mounted on the front, which made the whole truck vibrate—even before he fired the Beast's motor up.

"I think so," I said, trying to find a good footing on my duffel bag. There was a bit of morning dew on the window, but not enough to warrant turning on the wipers.

He put the manual transmission into gear and slowly let out the clutch as he juggled his cup of coffee between which hand had the least amount of activity.

Maneuvering a semi-truck with no power steering one handed was impressive. It was as if there was a trucker code which prevented him from sitting his coffee down in the cup holder. I held mine too, just in case.

On top of the stainless-steel travel mug he grasped with his hand like an eagle with its prey, he also had a backup thermos sitting on the floor next to his seat. It was an old-fashioned metal type with a plastic outer lid which was used as a cup and a smaller inner cap to keep the contents inside. The passage of time had removed much of the green paint and the bare-metal had many battle scars but what caught my attention was a king's crown engraved onto the side of it.

As the Beast rolled across the parking area, it surprised me by how much my chair, which had an air shock for suspension, bounced up and down.

It's not too late, I can still jump out. I can humbly tell him to stop the truck, politely excuse myself, and run like hell.

I focused on breathing deeply.

"Have you ever ridden in an eighteen-wheeler?" He smiled at my discomfort.

"I'll be fine. I just need to dig in some roots." Clipping my seatbelt, I tugged on it to be sure it was securely attached to the truck.

"This is gonna be a long trip. Tell me if you need to get out and stretch your legs." As he pulled up to the road, he put his left turn signal on.

Just one day. I can make it just one day.

"Where are we heading today?"

"Arizona, we have to drop off this load of potatoes."

"It's been a long while since I've been over there."

"I'm sorry, Bud, I don't believe I've caught your name."

"I'm Nathan."

"Nathan," he paused to take a swig off his mug, "that's not a very good trucker's name. I'm going to call you Bud."

"That's fine." I joined him with a sip, but I don't drink coffee. I drink brown sunshine. It's like the sun, always there to remind me that everything is okay. "What are these so-called steps?"

"They are some real-world stuff. Things you'll never hear from that fancy school of yours."

"And what's that?"

"I'm going to break it down into fifty-three simple little steps. We'll call them the Baby Steps. Follow them exactly as I tell them to you, and you'll probably be fine."

"Snow Queen Sally mentioned something about a Golden Step?" I sunk slightly, like a puppy wanting to go outside, but not wanting to annoy his master.

He looked me straight in the eye. "I don't teach that to just anyone."

"Why not?"

"Not everyone is prepared to accept the change in their lives which it will create."

"How so?"

"The Baby Steps alone could take their business to the next level. They are the things which are learned by experience, yet those with experience won't share."

"—and?"

"The Golden Step is much more than that. It not only changes how we look at business, but also how we look at life. It's the same as putting on a pair of sunglasses and noticing how everything looks darker. Only with the Golden Step, it makes the entire world brighter."

"Brighter?"

"It shines light on paths you may not have noticed. It makes decisions clear. It makes your entire reality a better experience."

"And some people are not ready for that?"

"No!" he snapped, maybe because of his temper—or because it disappointed him that the answer was true.

"Well, I appreciate whatever you are willing to teach me."

"Not a problem." The motor grunted as he let out on the clutch.

I returned to a mindful focus on my deep breathing.

*

"Pfff…" I spilled my brown sunshine down the front of my shirt. It turned out bringing extra clothes was a good idea.

After we got up to speed on the highway, the ride inside of the cab-over turned out to be very bumpy. My seatbelt kept locking in position and trying to choke me out. "How do you drink stuff while this thing is driving down the road?"

"I don't. That's what stop signs and intersections are for." Regardless, he dared not to set his coffee mug down.

"Tell me, when did you meet Snow Queen Sally?" I searched for a topic of which we both had in common.

"I can't say for sure exactly when I met her. It was a bit too long ago to remember. What I can say is that she was the glue that kept us all together."

"There was a group of you all?"

"A big one back then," he paused. "I remember a gathering at her place. My good buddies were scattered about the house, talking about old times, new times, and big trucks. Snow Queen Sally, Gravel Pit Gary—named that because he runs belly dump trailers—and I were in the kitchen shooting the bull.

"We were the only entrepreneurs of the group, and she was the newest member. I was helping her start her first venture, and we were doing well."

"What was it she was doing?"

"Snowplowing—of course."

"Of course."

"Business is more than merely sitting in an office, telling people to work harder, and dealing with mergers. For most people, it's finding what they can do well and getting it done.

"She figured she wanted to snowplow, so I helped her set up accounts, establish a strong financial foundation, and spread salt at four in the morning. It seems to me that spreading salt before dawn is more of what business is about than dealing with mergers."

"Yup, sounds right."

"She confided in Gravel Pit Gary and me, that she would get so stressed that sometimes she would get nauseous. I told her the story about when I had recently bought my rig and was trying to make it on my own. When I started out, I was barely making enough money for fuel." His face cringed noticeably. "I ended up living off of rice and cooked peas for most of the duration. I hated both of them before then, and now it is stronger than ever."

"That's agreeable."

"Most nights, I would shut off my rig, and instantly collapse into a deep sleep. If the day did not exhaust me enough for that to happen, then my mind would start thinking of the pressure to succeed and the obstacles I had until I would vomit.

"It took me about three months to gain enough ground financially so that I could afford proper food. I was almost twenty pounds lighter, but I was up and running. Gravel Pit Gary could match every story I had with a similar one of his own.

"Since that day when I hooked onto a trailer for the first time, I have started and ran many businesses. Over that period,

I made good money, lost it all, made it back, lost it all again and, finally, made it back.

"I have lived in my truck down by the river and slept on the concrete floor of someone's basement. I ate my share of rice and noodles—not to mention buying fuel with pocket change. This is the actual nature of business.

"That is why I believe most training courses are full of shit, pardon my language. They lie! They paint pictures that are all roses and when people set off after their fortunes, which were promised—they get slapped in the face. I have made my fortunes, but not in the same world as these self-proclaimed gurus describe.

"I have had my share of new houses, trucks, motorcycles, and everything else I desired. However, I think Henry David Thoreau said it best, 'The true cost of a thing is the amount of what I will call life which is required to be exchanged for it, immediately or in the long run.' My fortune didn't come freely."

"I wouldn't take you for the type of person to quote Thoreau."

Who am I with and what have I gotten myself into?

"That boy saved my life more than once," he exaggerated—maybe.

"Tell me more about the Baby Steps?"

"I asked myself, if any of my friends wanted to be entrepreneurs, what would I recommend to them? And so, I came up with these steps. It is what I would want my good friends to be aware of before they set off to change their lives.

"No fluff, no lies, and no painting pictures of luxury homes, magic wands, or pixie dust. Don't get me wrong, I want you to venture down this road of independence. I also want you to be aware of what lies ahead and equip yourself to handle it."

"The question I have is—if it is such a challenge, then why would anybody want to do it?"

"I could tell you the typical answers of independence and financial freedom—however, those are also lies. You'll eventually reach those points, but probably not during the first years of operation.

"You'll get all the independence you want—you only have to work twenty-four hours a day, seven days a week. The rest of the time is yours to do what you feel. You don't have to wait until noon to take lunch—you eat whenever you want. Or, to be more exact, whenever you can find the chance.

"I usually find lunch in a wrapper and eat it while multi-tasking. Even now I continue to work most waking hours of the day, seven days a week. However, I tend to take the winters off. I'm not a fan of driving in the snow."

"Don't blame you there."

"As for financial freedom, I remember talking to a lovely lady and bragging about how I broke even that year. I'm not sure if I impressed her, but the fact is, almost all businesses lose money initially. Most of them continue to lose money or break even in the following years. That is merely one reason so many fail during the initial years of operation. There are many more reasons we'll get to later."

"Really?"

"Yes. When I said that I broke even, I was mostly over the hump. Everything was going to go more smoothly now. Business is a long-term endeavor. Initially, you usually lose money because of startup costs, high operating expenses, and low income.

"During the second and third years, you might break even—if you're lucky. You'll have high operating costs, low income, and, if you financed your startup, then you'll have those to pay towards."

"This sounds tough."

"It's hard to describe how tough it really is. By the third year, you may slowly start developing a more solid foundation—you may actually be able to slip away for a week off, but you most likely won't be capable of doing any major purchases.

"After five years, you'll probably have more capital and be able to make major purchases when needed. Things might be a bit lean, though. I figure that possibly, after seven years or so, you might start getting some financial independence. This timeline is the average which I've observed, but it may change considerably with aggression, hard work, and luck."

"You're making me reconsider what I majored in school. Should I go back and switch it to midwestern postmodern art?"

"Let me put it to you this way, the decision to become an entrepreneur comes down to two simple reasons—first, it is the lesser of two evils, such as buying a house versus renting one.

"When you buy a house, roughly seventy percent of your first monthly mortgage payment is for interest. From there, it only gets slightly better. This is money thrown out the window. On top of that, you have property taxes and maintenance.

"However, as time goes by, or with improvements, your house goes up in value. Also, as time passes, less of your payment goes toward interest. This doesn't seem like a lot of pay off when considering the sacrifice. However, when you rent a home, all of your money goes out the window.

"All the improvements you do will definitely make your landlord happier. After a decade, when you move, the only equity you have will be your coffee table."

"I never thought of it that way."

"Likewise, working a normal job for somebody else is only going to earn them money. You'll have no more rights in the operation than the day you started. When you own a business, you build equity, same as a house—someday, you could have a sellable enterprise.

"It is nearly impossible to achieve economic independence while working for another person. Simply put, you might become wealthy, but you will always depend on them—you are their servant."

"Servant?"

"Also, when you own a business, your problems are your own—at a job, everyone's problems are your problems. You may enjoy your job, but everybody higher on the corporate ladder will trickle their issues down to you. It doesn't matter if it's personal, either. When you run your own business, you can simply fire all those people."

"And the second reason?"

"The second reason to become an entrepreneur is that it's an addiction. There are meetings for alcoholics and drug addicts—we need one for entrepreneurs. This might sound ridiculous, but if an alcoholic, a druggie, and an entrepreneur were all thinking of selling their TV to keep their habit going, I know which one would be the quickest to sell it."

"That sounds peculiar."

Seriously—what have I gotten myself into?

"I'm merely saying, if you talk to any entrepreneur about this, they'll bow their heads in shame because they know the truth. Would've I sold my TV so I could put fuel in my tank? Damn straight I would."

"Really?"

"It's like setting a tame horse loose in the wild. The problem is that it becomes wild again. After which, you can no longer break the horse of its nature. Most entrepreneurs can't keep a normal job because it isn't in their nature anymore. To them, when they work for somebody else, they are dead on the inside.

"They won't hesitate to sell their TV or live in their semi down by the river, if that's what it takes. I know this well. I have roamed the wild, tasted freedom—and no longer am I able to be treated as a caged animal."

This is why I am here.

Chapter Two

The Baby Steps

It's no mystery about why they stopped calling. I would steer the conversation back to them repeatedly until they realized I had nothing to say. I live inside my bedroom playing video games and watching TV. Stopped taking a shower every day, then lost track of them all together. I know it's time to take one when I touch my hair and my hands get tacky. That might sound bad, but it's easy to do when there's nothing to mark the day.

They are on social media. I see their new jobs, new cars, and new girlfriends, but I've stopped calling them, too. Am I really so worthless that I would risk my life and travel with a complete stranger, really hoping that maybe he might know an answer? Worthless? Pathetic? I guess I shouldn't ask questions I don't want answers to.

"What are the Baby Steps about?" I asked the Oracle to silence the glum goblin that lived in my head.

Arizona as a whole is not a barren wasteland, but parts of it certainly are. Driving through northern Arizona at sixty-two miles per hour was torturous. We burned through almost an entire audiobook since the last time we had seen civilized civilization.

"Well," he said as he reached over and turned down the audiobook, "common sense would say that they would be a to-do list, an instruction manual claiming—follow in my footprints, and you may get what you desire. Wake up, comb your hair, drive your tank to work, and so on—just do as I do.

"Unfortunately, we cannot describe the full complexity of the business world in an instruction manual. They are much more than a *do this* and *have that*. To be successful, you must first *be*, then *do* and *have* will follow."

"I don't understand."

"I've had the fortune of being good friends with a very wealthy man named Oil Rig Otis. He started out with a meager oil tanker truck, but wanted a bigger piece of the pie. Though he began with only one oil rig, it quickly became two, then twenty, then an oil refinery and eventually his own oil empire. He said that if he lost everything, and was still in his youth, he could rebuild it all in a few years."

"Okay," I said as I tried to follow along.

"Despite what he had done to become successful, his strength was mostly due to *who* he was. It was his *being* that made his wealth and would allow him to recapture it if needed. The Baby Steps are guides on what *being* looks like."

"You're saying that with success, the *doing* part is actually not what I should focus on?"

"Correct. After you develop your *being*—the *doing* and the *having* will follow like second nature. This will make you the leader that the world you dominate needs."

"Well said."

Baby Step #1

"Number one!" the Oracle said loudly, riding that fine line between excitement and aggression.

My body jolted, almost causing me to spill my brown sunshine, "What?"

After turning south at Tuba City—Arizona magically became even more boring. The Oracle could've put a stick through the steering wheel, jumped out of the Beast, and it would've been an hour before it ran off the road. To make things worse—he forgot to turn back on the audiobook from our last conversation.

"I'm about to say something that you might disagree with, but I would like you to hear my case first. Not all MLM businesses are bad."

"A what?"

"I guess to describe what an MLM, multi-level marketing, network marketing, or whatever else they decide to call it, I need to start off at the beginning. It started as what they call a pyramid scheme. That's an organization saying that, for five hundred dollars, you can join our team.

"Next, you go out and persuade others to join the program. When you sign a new member, you collect a cut of the sign-up fees they pay.

"After they convince others to join, they'll receive a portion of the newbies sign-up fees—and you'll also get a reduced amount of this cash, and so forth until you are getting small pieces from the thousands and thousands of people in your down-line."

"Sounds reasonable."

"The problem is that there is no product. You are selling nothing other than the right to collect money—all the hard-working folks at the bottom of this huge pyramid will lose their asses because they are the profit. Needless to say, they are illegal."

"Then what is the difference between a pyramid scheme and an MLM?"

"It is still a pyramid scheme, but with a product. These are legal because they aim to earn a profit by selling actual products, not solely by signing people up and charging monster fees."

"Still sounds shady…"

"You're right, some of them are not much better than their illegal cousin. Those with a basement full of water softeners or seven thousand dollars in vitamins will probably agree."

"You're saying that it is merely a pyramid scheme in disguise?"

"Let me put it to you this way. I was talking to the local gym owner, and he said that the first of the year is a great time because of those joining as New Year's resolutions. Every year, I avoid going there the first three days of the year—it is crowded until day four and then returns to normal. It's a sad fact, but it's true.

"The owner said that he actually loses cash from the people who come regularly—they wear out the equipment sooner. Where he brings in his profit is from those who register, usually paying annually, and then only appearing a few times before giving up."

"That also sounds shady…"

"I'm sure that those MLM organizations would be more than glad to sell you more vitamins if you did, by chance, sell all seven grand worth. I still say that they are more interested in signing up those who have a fistful of cash instead of a nutrient deficiency and a desire to run their own business.

"The higher the sign-up fee is, the more it resembles a pyramid scheme. All the poor suckers on bottom are the ones losing money."

"If you're wanting me to join one, then you're not selling it very well."

"Some are not that bad. As a rule of thumb, I would never pay more than a couple hundred dollars to join one, and that's only if I really believed in the product.

"There are many that you can join for under a hundred bucks, however. These operations don't break a profit unless you buy or sell their products. To be honest, I am an emerald level member of the Lexatez Industries organization."

"What? Is this a sales pitch?"

"No, but let me explain why I'm part of such an organization."

"I'm listening."

"With Lexatez and most of these other outfits, you'll lose your investment. Even though it only has a small sign-up fee, they'll con you into buying their merchandise.

"They sell such products as phone cards or toilet paper that can be ordered online and delivered to your doorstep. They sell pretty much everything that local chain stores do and while the product may be decent, they are still heavily overcharging."

"What is a phone card?"

"They typically sell them in gas stations and they are a prepaid card so you can call others long distance."

"Long distance?"

"This was before free long distance on cell phone plans. I assume they still make them?"

"Never paid attention to them. I suppose it was before my time."

"Well, the reason I mention this type of venture is that for those that have never tasted the freedom of their own enterprise, they have, hands down, the fastest, cheapest, and easiest way to obtain hands-on business training, regardless of where they live, and that is why I am an emerald member."

"That's odd."

"Real estate offers better in-depth training, but it most likely wouldn't make sense. Most states require between ninety to three hundred hours of schooling, passing a state exam, and the thousands in startup costs by joining an office and buying a day planner. As a career, it might be a good idea only if you intend to pursue it seriously.

"Otherwise, an MLM might be the best way to go. With Lexatez Industries, they may submerge themselves in the business realm for only the seventy-eight-dollar sign-up fee, and before I drive off, I make sure that they know to not actually buy many of the products.

"The bigger the organization, the more likely it is that they offer free, or nearly free, training meetings and seminars. Lexatez has seminars weekly."

"Just don't get sucked in too deeply?"

"Exactly. Not only will they teach you the fundamentals, but you get to observe what others are doing and what is working for them. They contain many professionals inside the organization who are glad to tutor you for free.

"All you need to do is pretend that you give a damn about the product. After you've milked the training for all it's worth, simply quit paying the annual fee. All the people will magically go away."

"Poof, they're gone," I said with a single clap of my hands.

"If you actually do attempt to earn a little dough this way, at least you wouldn't owe on a thirty-year business loan. While some who join actually make money, the fools at the lowest level still seem to get crapped on. Wait until you open your first check for forty-eight cents. Even after a year, mine only come to a couple of bucks a month."

"They've paid me less at some jobs I've worked at before."

Lies! I've never had an actual job. I still eat whatever groceries are in the cupboard and hit my mom up whenever I need some cash. These little lies are a mask I need to wear for now.

"It is not because of the business structure that more people don't rake in the cash—it is because of a flaw in the system that causes them to quit."

"What's that?"

"The flaw is that they talk you into attending the meetings, and the speakers there make you so excited that it's hard to stay in your chair. Then, after getting wound up, you run out the door ecstatic like a child.

"However, when you get a big fat 'NO!' from the first person you try to get to join—you fall flat on your face. Why? Excitement is weak and lacks the conviction needed to carry you through the hard parts."

"Excitement is weak?"

I wish my day had excitement in it. I'm becoming unfamiliar with that experience.

"This, unfortunately, is the common thread of those who start out on their own, MLM or otherwise. Real estate agents get ecstatic when they score their own cubicle, and a sort of excitement knowing that they possess this power of being able to sell a house!

"After twenty cold calls, they stop calling. After three failed sales right before closing, they go back to their jobs at the pizza parlor.

"What about when you need to sell your TV to get gas money? How about your boat? Will excitement carry you on when you have to sell your house? Can you truly be that excited about selling online toilet paper?" he asked.

"I don't know how to answer that."

"Imagine you're a hundred and twenty years old, on your death bed—what is it you wish you had done? What are you truly passionate about? Is it working your way up the corporate ladder towards a pension at the Mervercon Corporation? Is it selling houses? Is it selling online toilet paper or soap? Probably not.

"To tell the truth—" he took a sip of coffee, "I don't care about Mervercon, if people use toilet paper, or live in a hut out in the forest. It's harsh, but, at more than a century old, I simply wouldn't feel strongly about such things.

"Passion is the long-term driving force found in any strong entrepreneur. Do you think a boat would stand in your way of accomplishing something you are passionate about?"

"How big of a boat are we talking?" This appeared as if I was a smartass, but it was a serious question.

"Musicians are the most passionate artists I can think of. If they had to look back at their success, do you think that having to sell their houses would stop them?

"Passion is not merely about achieving greatness—it is about something that you would rather do more than breathe, eat, or sleep. Could it be selling online toiletries? Who am I to say what moves you? Obviously, some like it enough to make a living at it."

"The online toilet paper business—what moves you for what moves you?" For this I did mean to come off as a smartass.

"The question I have for you is—how can you make a living doing what you are the most passionate about?"

Chapter

Three

Baby Step #2

"Well, if it isn't my friend Jimmy Z and the King," the lady in the faded turquoise waitress uniform asked the Oracle as she smiled at him.

There were four upside down standard issue brown ceramic coffee cups on our table. Both of us flipped a cup over and she filled them.

"My name is Bud," I said almost inaudibly.

I took a mouthful of my brown sunshine, knowing well that it was too hot. It was something that needed to be done in order to fit in the two creamers and three sugar packets—and at this hour, there was no time to waste.

"The King is his thermos—kid," she corrected me.

It was odd that he brought it into a diner, but then again, I hadn't seen him separated from it yet.

"You named your thermos after Elvis?"

"Did I?" He peered at me with no expression on his face.

"What'll you have, hon? The usual?"

The Oracle's Golden Step

"Yep."

"And what about for the kid?" She looked over at me.

"I would like an order of fries—could I also get a side of mayonnaise?" I put my menu down, well, what menu there was. It was written on a large piece of paper that served as a placemat to eat on.

"Mayonnaise and fries?" She stopped writing on her pad.

"I make my own fry sauce by mixing it with ketchup."

"Sure deal."

"How old is this place?" I asked.

"Can't say. Route 66 used to flow through here, so I think they built it back then." She turned and walked away.

They designed the whole restaurant similar to a huge train car, mainly rectangular but curved at the corners. A few feet from the ceiling was a shelf built around the entire inner diameter of it, in which a model train circled round and round as if needing to make the daily deliveries.

I assumed that someone built the old hotel behind the restaurant around the same time. I was wrong in assuming that since the Beast didn't have sleeping quarters we would be returning home every night. Hotel life suited me fine.

"You bring enough money for this trip?"

"Why do you ask?"

Is he hinting about whether I'm willing to pitch in for the night's accommodations? Eek... Maybe I can have my mom send me more money.

"It's dinnertime, and you only ordered some fries."

"I didn't just order fries—I also ordered a side of mayonnaise. But, yes, money will be tight."

"You came on this trip with barely enough money to make it?"

"How I saw it was that I had two possible futures and, depending on what decision I made, would define who I was. One option was to return to my parent's house and spend my summer playing video games and wasting away.

"The other was to come on this journey and eat toast for breakfast, chips or crackers for lunch, and fries for dinner. It seems there's never enough money to do the things we desire. I could be the person who stays at home because he wants to be comfortable, or I could be the person who seeks great adventures. I decided I wanted to show up for life."

More lies. Show up for life? Yes. Great adventures? That's a stretch.

"Fair enough. I can get your dinner if you want something more than that."

"I'm grateful you invited me to come along and the choices I made shouldn't affect you."

"It's not a big deal. I don't intend to see you starve."

"I suspect I'll make it off bread and fries fine, but thanks for the offer."

"That brings me to," he paused and looked around, then shouted, "number two!"

"Two!" I returned the excitement.

"But wait—Dharma!" he called over at the waitress.

"Yes, hon?" She hurried over.

"You want to sit in on this?"

I scooted over on my booth seat to provide room for her out of politeness.

"Of course, I just love the way you talk," she said as she flipped another coffee mug over and filled it before she sat down. "Fifty-two years of questionable decisions brought me here. Seems like I'm old enough to make better decisions in my life."

I wondered if the heat was going to damage the table when she put the nearly full coffee pot on it.

"The dollar bill has no more actual worth than the toilet paper you buy online," he said like school was now in session. "Cash represents a medium used for exchange, but it has no other function or value. It is merely an illusion of worth.

"Before major corporations, capitalism, and the New York stock exchange—when chickens still roamed the open streets— folks would go to the market to trade eggs for milk, meat for bread, and so on. Since there were no refrigerators or plastic wrap then, that trip was for most a daily ordeal."

The smell of fryer grease and cheap cigarettes from Dharma distracted me momentarily.

"To simplify the barter system, they started using coins made of precious metals, particularly gold and silver. Then they could swap their eggs for valuable coins, and then trade the coins for bread, for example. They later printed paper money and made coins out of recycled beer cans and other non-precious metals.

"If only empty beer cans were actually cash, my deadbeat husband Dwayne would be wealthy and I wouldn't have to work here no more," Dharma said sarcastically.

"They made the paper money and cheap coins to represent a certain quantity of gold," he said. "Today, about eighteen hundred of these paper dollars is equal to one ounce of the shiny stuff. For every dollar and coin in circulation, there had to be that much gold stashed away. In the early 1970s, they increased the amount of bills printed beyond what could be covered by what they had stored in the vault.

"You're saying that the value of money is make believe now?" I asked.

"Sort of. Cash just represents a quantity of exchange and has no more worth than play money. It is the eggs and bread that are valuable. To have goals based merely on the acquisition of this fake wealth is ridiculous. It's like individuals who take playing games too seriously and ruin it for everybody else."

"It's most likely the same people who don't leave a tip," she sought to add to the conversation.

"Probably, however, today there is no other major method of exchange. Some form of currency is now almost an essential part of our daily trip to the market. You would get strange looks if you went to the supermarket to trade gold for milk or eggs."

"Or like trying to pay for your meal at a restaurant with live chickens?" she giggled.

"Exactly. The reason I brought up the point of money as an illusion of worth is that if you take it too seriously, there could be mild catastrophic ramifications.

"When you are a hundred and twenty years old and on your death bed, great riches probably won't mean as much to you as the way you spent your life. I have been good friends with many happy wealthy people and with many unhappy wealthy people. The unhappy ones failed to find passion in their professions and quite possibly their lives as a whole."

"That's deep," I said.

"When I was fresh out of high school and everything in this world was new to me, I took a night job vacuuming the floors at a local real estate office.

"There was an agent who made about half a million yearly in sales. He had his own wing of the office for all the staff who worked with him.

"As you entered his part of the building, you would pass his secretary's desk, which had a candy dish full of muscle relaxers and antidepressants for his team members."

"That must've been tempting for a teenager, alone with a bowl full of that stuff," she said.

"Even in those days, I knew it took more than it gave."

"Well put." I was a little surprised by his answer.

"Not that I wasn't around it a lot. This is a common story, and I could go on with many more involving secretaries vomiting in the drinking fountain from too much whiskey or CEOs wearing suits in the day and snorting coke at night.

"The truth is, most of the agents I knew in that typical real estate office were alcoholics—some of them did drugs. Almost everyone had a bottle of something in the top drawer of their desk. As I was coming in for the evening, I would often see them raid the pop machine to mix drinks. Rarely would I notice them making it through a full day before doing this.

"Once they gave the habit up, their career only lasted a little longer. I imagine that's how they managed the stress of it."

"That's dark. Are you saying all real estate agents are druggies and alcoholics?"

"There were some who worked sober and actually enjoyed it. They worked in moderation and had a deep passion for helping others. But some are in it for the money and don't care if people live in caves. Hopefully they were rarer than I remember."

"I'd make a cave my home if I was able to call it my own," she mentioned.

I suspected she was serious.

"Speaking of it, one of my good friends used to live in one. His name was Super Ego, but we called him Id. I met him about twelve thousand years ago. He was a decent guy, not complex at all.

"To Id's reptilian brain, there were only things that would increase his chance of survival or decrease his chance of death. Even though they are basically the same statements, his brain treated them separately. To run from a dinosaur would decrease his chance of death—eating it would increase his chance of living."

"Sometimes Jimmy Z gets a bit creative," she said over at me.

"I've noticed."

"To ease the strain of analyzing every action, whether it would lead to life or death," he continued, "the brain created two emotions—pleasure and strife. To push you away from death, our minds created strife or pain. Pleasure is for things that will increase the chances of survival.

"Pain and pleasure are illusions, just the same as money. Money equals exchange, pleasure equals life, pain equals death. Everything we are motivated to do is because it will ultimately improve our prospects of living or lower our chances of death, as considered by our minds."

"As considered by our minds?" I asked.

"I say it that way because, sometimes, the signals get complicated or confused. One argument is that someone may smoke cigarettes because they have somehow linked more pleasure than pain to it."

"You're speaking to the choir, hon." Dharma coughed almost as if on cue.

"Well, you, for instance, additionally now have the agony of quitting attached to it. Until there is more pleasure and less pain attained by not smoking, stopping for long-term will be a constant fight against the primal reptilian brain."

"You're saying there's no chance of me ever giving it up?"

"I'm saying to quit, tip the scale. A therapist, for instance, might link enormous amounts of pain to smoking or enormous amounts of pleasure to being smoke-free.

"Once you tip the scales, it will simply be a matter of time before you quit and a natural gravity will draw you to being free from cigarettes. After all, we perceive pleasure in what ultimately pulls us towards survival."

"Hmmm…" she replied.

"When you have more pain than pleasure associated with a job, your primal instinct is to stay in bed every morning. Once you lose the satisfaction that took you down the road to begin with, you are fighting your instincts. It is the same as having a huge dinosaur chase you."

"That makes sense," she finally agreed.

"This will be the ninth-year doing long haul. When I started, I had to seclude myself inside my truck's cabin with no TVs or radio allowed. I had to do that because, even though I got some gratification from driving, I received more joy from watching movies and it's not safe to do both at the same time."

"Is the cab big enough for a television set?"

"I used to carry a portable DVD unit that had a tiny screen on it, but I no longer travel with it. By getting rid of these temptations, I was left with either driving or being bored. The open road won out.

"Now, I drive while all my distraction devices rest peacefully at home—I have attached more satisfaction to grabbing a few extra miles than watching a good movie. Sometimes, if I feel the need to catch up on a sitcom when I'm somewhere with a TV, I can use discomfort to give me the focus I need to return to my work. I might remind myself of a deadline, or how much money I'm losing in order to sit there."

"Idle hands make empty paychecks."

"Another thing that I must point out—the brain favors avoiding pain over gaining pleasure. Id would most likely run from the dinosaur rather than to try to eat it.

"Dharma, what motivated you most when you started working at this job? Was it the fear of living in a cardboard box under a tree? Was it starving to death? Or was it because you really wanted to work and enjoyed it?"

"Here? You know I'm irresistibly drawn to fried food," she smirked, which caused her to cough again.

"Pain may easily be the best short-term motivator, but pleasure has a tendency to win in the long run. In my experience, people go to college not because of the dread of living in a mediocre shack, but because they want the enjoyment of doing something with their lives. However, it's feasible that they really do need a big house.

"They might start college because they are fed up with their current circumstances, but the ones who stay at it are those that have the long-term gratification of success in mind."

"That explains my education loans," I said.

"When you find passion for what you do, it doesn't mean that there won't still be times you think working at your business sucks. All jobs suck every so often. That's what makes it a profession instead of merely a hobby.

"Being passionate about what you do means that you still link more happiness to it and you won't quit merely because of a bad day. You have more of the good brain stuff attached to it than the boat that you have to sell to keep going. When you find that passion, you will be unstoppable."

"Your orders up." Dharma excused herself to go get our food.

Baby Step #3

"Number three!"

"Three!"

Our empty plates were littered across the top of the table at the diner and our brown sunshine no longer had the heat to bellow steam. Our bellies were full and our waitress had run off to help other customers.

I found it strange that he ate chili for breakfast and eggs, ham, bacon, toast and a single pancake for dinner. However, it did describe the man.

"Values are the shades of pain and pleasure that color the emotional world."

"Well said—though what do my valuables have to do with that?"

"Not valuables—values," he chuckled. "Values are emotional states that are variations of pain and pleasure. Though, ultimately, they are used to move you away from death and towards life.

"Some values that are death repellents would be fear, anger, and rejection. Some that are life magnets would be joy, acceptance, and security—for instance."

"I see, but you forgot to mention money."

"Money is not a value and never will be. In physical terms, money has no actual worth except what it represents—the exchange of money for goods."

"So, it goes back to the ancient marketplace." I took a sip of my lukewarm brown sunshine. "You're saying it is meaningless?"

"Sort of, it is a *vehicle* our mind uses to bring us to an emotional state. Money may rid you of the fear of starvation or being rejected by others, or it may bring the joy of buying what you want or the security of making your house payment on time. Money has some purpose, but no one has ever done anything of significant accomplishment solely for the money."

"No one?"

"Okay, perchance a few, in all fairness."

"If it wasn't for money, most people wouldn't leave their houses."

"Well, the line between what they would consider a value or what would be a value-vehicle that brings us a value may be blurred somewhat.

"We should consider work and play as vehicles, but, for all intents and purposes of this Baby Step, we may revise them as values. After all, struggle and sweat are something to consider heavily before pursuing a path."

"You're right. When I accept a certain direction, I don't think I reflect on the required effort as deeply as I should. Such as when I signed up for college, I had this vision of what life would be like with that diploma.

"I knew it would demand some effort, but the labor was so overshadowed by the desire in my head that it was hard to take into full consideration."

"Dharma..." The Oracle caught our waitress's attention as she ran by us.

"Yes, hon?"

"You have a pen and paper I can borrow?"

"Oh, I already have a pen and I can use the other side of the menu. It's paper. I doubt they reuse it." I pulled out my generic ballpoint that I cut down to roughly three inches—barely long enough to write with, but small enough to fit into the front pocket of my pants.

"That's good. I only have the one I use to take orders with. You boys need anything else?"

"No—thanks," he said to the back of her head as she ran off.

"Thank you," I also said to be polite, even though I'm sure she didn't hear.

"Why do you have a miniature pen?"

"I learned to always carry one. You never know when you'll get a girl's number—better to be prepared."

"Smart, maybe you should be the soothsayer."

"If a girl actually ever wants to give me her digits, then I don't want to miss the opportunity."

I moved my coffee mug over to my left hand so I could hold the pen with my right. Setting my brown sunshine on the table wasn't an option at this time of night.

"We should list effort, combined with stress, as a moving away value. Stress is easy to see as a value because it is, after all, an emotional state. However, you should consider labor because in the long run, you want to reap a sufficient reward for your struggles."

"What about the things that bring enjoyment? You know, the good stuff in life, like this—" I held up my mug and took another sip. By now, it was so cold that adding creamer most likely would have warmed it up.

"We can consider having a good time as a value-vehicle because it brings us to joy or relaxation and such, depending on how we have fun. If you play as if you are a child in your spare moments, then I see no harm in using it on your list.

"Men have more of a tendency to act like children. As a man, I understand the importance of it."

"Same."

"If you consider sitting by a lake with a fishing pole important, then perhaps you should put relaxation on your list."

"I've lured a creature of lesser intelligence onto a fish hook myself."

"You might notice that some values, being simply shades of pain and pleasure, are similar in meaning. Joy and happiness, worry and stress, and so on, are similar in nature. You can use either, unless each has a unique meaning to you. Stress for me includes worry but also may include anger."

"Should I worry about my safety around you?" I joked, but not really. "It seems as if there's a massive amount of confusion about what is deemed a value."

"What is classified as a value, verses what is actually a value-vehicle is not always black and white. There is certainly a lot of vagueness about the meanings of these words. Numerous books have attempted to list and describe them, with little agreement among them."

"Alright, I'm doing my best to follow along here. You say what is a value versus being a value-vehicle is subjective. There are no strongly definable boundaries between the two. Then why even distinguish them? Why are they important anyhow?

What does any of this have to do with business?" I tossed my pen onto the table.

"I think it's time to break out the back side of that menu."

"Fine…" I pouted as I grabbed my pen.

"Write as many values that you can come up with that influence your life. It is essential for you to do this because they are the foundation of passion. Therefore, much of these Baby Steps will revolve around these simple exercises." He took a drink off from what now must've been cold coffee.

"Fair enough."

I struggled to write the list the best that I could. It was still somewhat unclear about what was actually classified as what. I had to pause with each one I wrote and ask myself if it was truly a value or if it was something that brought me to one.

In the end, my list resembled a PG-13 romance novel with a lot of sappy words. This did not look like a business exercise.

"There, done—I think."

"Are you sure these are emotional states, or are they vehicles to bring you to one?"

"To the best of my ability, they are."

"Very well then. Let me ask, do these words have heartfelt meaning for you? Do they have significant importance to you? This is the primary issue at hand."

"I believe they are important."

"Write the *moving away* and *moving toward* values in separate columns. Put them in order of which ones you feel are most influential to you. If you have over ten in each column, then make a top ten list."

"It's like a cheat sheet for fulfillment in life?"

"You could consider it that way. I avoid journeying to places that won't lead me to my top moving toward values. Furthermore, I try to defuse the power that the top moving away values have over me. Look over it and ask yourself—is this list a blueprint to your passion?"

Is this the answer I'm looking for? There has to be more...

Chapter Four

Baby Step #4

"Number four!"

"Four!"

Smoke billowed through the restaurant in the search of innocent lungs to corrupt. All the staff, from the fry cooks to the late shift manager, had a cigarette clinging to their dry lips as they toiled away on their end of day tasks. A radio in the kitchen blasted the golden oldies.

Dharma locked the doors, turned off the outside lights, flipped the sign to closed, and then sat next to me. She lit a long thin cigarette and held it between her two fingers, as if she was classier than the others. On the table were three freshly poured cups of coffee and an ashtray that she had stashed away until after closing time.

"Dharma, you said that a lifetime of poor decisions led you to this job. What did you mean by that?"

"Who and where I am today is a result of the choices I made twenty years ago, ten years ago, five years ago, and yesterday. I could've moved out of this town, gone to college, tried a little harder at some of my jobs…" She took a puff off her smoke. "So many possibilities, and yet somehow here I am."

"Precisely," the Oracle said, "and who and where we will be in the days to come will result from the conclusions we arrive at today. By understanding that you are who you are because of the decisions you made in the past gives you great power to control the outcome of your future.

"You live where you live because at some point you said yes to living there. You work where you work because at some point you thought it would be the best thing for you. Your relationships with others are a certain way because you determined you wanted them in your life. Your decisions created all the problems you deal with every day."

"Hold on—not everything in my life is my fault. You need to take into consideration good old-fashioned bad luck sometimes."

"Some ramifications of your decisions are obvious, while some may require some abstract thinking. It is clear that by sending in a credit card application and buying a new car, your finances trapped you, forcing you to stick at a job you hate."

"That's understandable," she said.

"You may say that you never caused your high school boyfriend to cheat, but you picked him over all others—now he has left you and you are stuck with your second option, marrying Dwayne.

"If you had picked a different option, such as going after the class nerd instead of the guy with the chromed-out hog, you wouldn't own an empty beer can collection. Or, perhaps after high school, you moved to another town where you met a different person who was maybe nicer—or maybe not."

"I guess Dwayne is nice enough. He just has his moods. I could've done worse."

"You're right, maybe you would've been worse off if you went down a different path. Maybe you would've attracted the same things, regardless of where you live, because of deep-rooted issues only you and eight years of therapy may discover."

"More like twenty…"

"I do not point this out to place the blame on anybody or make you depressed. By saying that you had no influence on where you are now, you also admit that you hold no power over where you are heading.

"You cannot believe you are a victim of circumstance while maintaining that you have control over your future. Victims don't see how their choices shape their current situation, so they won't understand how it will alter their destiny."

"You're saying there's no such thing as bad luck?" she snapped.

Some of those words are cutting into me, too.

"Bad things do happen now and probably also in the days ahead, but I do believe that both positive and negative thoughts attract relative results. In order for that thought to be formed and repeated, at some point, you reached a conclusion and unknowingly accepted it.

"By saying, *all these bad things resulted from judgments I made in the past, and negative thinking attracted bad luck*, you can also say, *I can make better ones today, which will make tomorrow brighter. By implementing positivity, things will go my way more often.*"

"Where you are today is a result of fate, not your past choices," a man who had gauged ear piercings, interrupted as he was wiping down the day's dirty tables and eavesdropping.

"I find that statement more disturbing than simply being accountable for myself. To say that it is ultimately destiny that controls your life is to say that you have no free will.

"No matter what you do, you are trapped by where it was predetermined for you to end up. Free will would only be an illusion because you were supposed to make those decisions—you did not choose them."

"That's a pretty deep philosophy." I quickly took a gulp of my brown sunshine. Talk too much, drink too little, you end up with a cold coffee. I will not learn that lesson twice.

"Let me break this down," he kept pace with the chugging of brown nectar, "classical scientists and philosophers conceived the notion of destiny centuries ago. In the world of classical physics, when an apple falls off a tree, gravity attracts it to the earth. Therefore, rules such as Sir Isaac Newton's laws of motion exist.

"They are called laws because people believed that—if this happened, then that would always happen. It would be so accurate that they could calculate it.

"The entire universe was simply a predictable machine with gears, pendulums, and pistons. Measuring a ball's trajectory rate and velocity, they knew exactly where the ball would land. Thus, they were predicting its fate, so to speak."

"I just did a double shift, hon, and I'm real tired. You might want to dumb that down a little." Being a woman of many chemicals, she took a swig of coffee, followed by another drag off her smoke.

"Classical scientists speculated that all the infinite universe was predictably moving by action and reaction. They had faith that, as soon as they discovered all laws of physics, they could find all the forces affecting the world.

"This means that they could figure out what was going to happen next. They believed it was only so long before the infinite future could be predicted with a calculator."

"I never considered it that way. That's interesting." The skin on the front of my forehead scrunched noticeably.

"This predictable future could also be called destiny, same as the falling apple hitting the ground. If this was true, then with a computer big enough, they could print a copy of every detail of your life from the moment you were born until you push up daisies. Fortunately, two major discoveries changed this way of thinking.

"The first was the discovery of modern physics at the turn of the twentieth-century. It said that the universe was far more complicated than we originally thought. It is more than simply gears and laws.

"Many modern physicists have admitted to using mind-altering drugs to wrap their heads around the strange universe of quantum mechanics."

"I'm going to need mind-altering drugs just to wrap my head around this conversation." She flicked the ash off the tip of her cigarette.

"The second reason," he continued, "in 1927, Heisenberg shattered the concept of a predestined future by his Uncertainty Principle. For classical scientists to predict your life, they would need to know all the factors affecting it, and figure them out altogether, in tandem. Heisenberg found two measurements that he wasn't able to calculate simultaneously."

"How?" I asked.

"You can whip out your calculator and measure an automobile's speed, or you can determine its exact position. However, you can't compute these simultaneously. It still remains impossible today."

"Again, how is that possible?"

"Without diving too far into physics, because, after all, these Baby Steps are about business, we could say that they found a trade-off.

"If they knew the vehicle's speed, they could estimate within an area of where it *probably* would be located. This launched the field of probabilities—which declares that nothing in this world is certain. However, we can figure out the *probability* of it happening."

"The probability of me forgetting this entire conversation is great," she said sarcastically.

"Let me try to say this another way. If an apple falls from a tree, a scientist back in 1859 would say that it certainly would hit the ground—today they can only assign an odd to it.

"There is an actual chance that before it reaches the earth, it will turn into a green monster and no scholar may dispute it. However, it is most likely that the apple will continue to fall as normal and life will go on."

"If there's such a high chance of it hitting the ground, couldn't you merely say that it was destined to?" I asked.

"Sort of, but not really. It's still feasible to take our calculators and assign odds towards whether something will or will not happen."

"Like my bookie?" she asked.

"Sort of, but typically with much larger numbers. The apple turning into a monster wouldn't hold very good odds—it would be about one to nine billion trillionth of a chance."

"Yup, same likelihood as my football team winning a game." She took a small puff.

"Chances are that with those odds there would be little that you could do to influence the outcome. If you can turn an apple into a monster before it hits the ground, it would impress me."

"It still sounds like the essence of destiny?"

"It might seem somewhat similar to it because some outcomes won't be probable, no matter how much you wish them to happen.

"The universe also has many outcomes in life that have better possibilities. If you came to a fork in the road, you would have a fifty-fifty chance of traveling down either side. These you've got complete control over.

"The more unlikely something appears to be, the more effort that might be required to accomplish it—although it is still a choice. People do continue to fly to the moon, after all."

"Do they?" she asked.

"I mention all of this because, with every fork in the road or conclusion you make, you change all the things that will probably happen to you in the future."

"Like getting stuck working at a diner when you're fifty-two years old?" she said as though she understood it.

"Exactly."

"This all sounds good in theory, but how does it apply to the business world?" I asked.

"The entrepreneur isn't solely a truck driver, salesman, salt spreader, hard worker, speaker, motivator, expert, and a numbers pusher—they are foremost, a decision maker.

"It is their job to call all the shots from the second they wake until they go to bed. This will bring them closer to their desires of being successful and leading a business into profitability."

"That seems to be a tremendous amount of pressure for a person." I finished the last of my cup of brown sunshine like a frat guy at a toga party.

"They are, after all, the captain at the helm of their enterprise. With every decision, no matter how small, they steer their vessel towards their target. Not only do they need to figure out how to bring in money, ensuring short-term success, but they also need to make certain that the direction they travel is in sync with their values, which will most likely lead to longer-term fulfillment."

"How do you deal with having so many decisions to make? I mean, not only do you have all the usual considerations, you also have one's such as which load to take. It seems as if a truck driver has an endless number of possibilities that may either be profitable or lose money."

"Yes, there are. For the small, everyday issues to consider, I trust that my unconscious mind will effortlessly guide me towards success. This is because I am clear on my value hierarchy and my ultimate aim inside my head. Plus, I consciously try to be more positive in my thoughts. This is a benefit of getting your unconscious working in harmony with your ambitions."

"What about for the bigger ones? Such as when to buy a new truck? Perhaps one with power steering?"

"First, I ask myself—what are the best actions or considerations for the life of the business?

"Then I consider, *is it in harmony with my top values in the short run?* Finally, *Down the road, in the long term, will it still be in alignment with most of my values?*"

"Ah! That's why you had me jot my values down on a piece of paper."

"That is one reason. There are many other ways that the list becomes useful."

"As in?"

"When I've got a couple of minutes to focus on it, there is a technique I've used for the past decade or so. It has served me well."

"Now we are getting to the good stuff," she pulled another cigarette out and lit it.

"Before I make up my mind on any major consideration," he said, "begin a new project, or open a new business, I make a grid. Here, let me see your paper."

"Ok." I slid it over and handed him my tiny pen.

He struggled to draw straight lines, but I suspected the undersized writing instrument in his large fingers had something to do with that.

"There," he said as he pushed it back over to me. "At the edge of each of the horizontal lines, put down one of your top ten *moving toward* and *moving away* values on each line."

I looked down at my list of values that I'd written on the back of my menu and copied it to his grid as instructed.

"Beside your most important values, write numbers between one and fifteen. Create a number between one and ten next to all the rest of the values listed."

"Okay," I said, trying to concentrate on the project.

"List some other things along with the values to be considered, such as if it's legal, may require strong physical strength, or require you to live with an in-law. List these if you think they are considerable influences and write a number between one and ten next to them."

"Okay."

"What are some of the current feats you're considering?" he asked.

"I've debated whether to set up a small business now while I am living with my family. Possibly a small motorcycle repair shop, a landscape business, a window cleaning company, or call me old-fashioned, but I've always dreamed of running a small video store."

"Then, turn the menu sideways. On the vertical lines, write a summary of each achievement to be considered."

"My grandkids write better than you do," Dharma said.

"I see on the top line you wrote—start a motorcycle shop. Go down on your grid to the first value to consider, which according to your list is freedom.

"Then ask yourself, on a scale of one to fifteen, how much freedom would you enjoy by starting one? It would be necessary to work many hours, which would hurt that.

"However, on the weekends, you would own a collection of bikes to ride, which would add to it. So, in your opinion, what score would you give that?"

"I would say that freedom would get a fourteen."

"Find the box on the grid that lines up *start a motorcycle shop* and *freedom* and put in the number twelve. Then go down the grid, asking that same question for each value."

"Will do." As I filled in each column for everything up for consideration and crossed them with how they affect each value, I noticed each of them becoming clearer.

"Now add up all the numbers in each decision column. You will have a series of numbers at the bottom. Each of them represents a verdict—the higher the amount, the more you should benefit from this choice."

"That seems logical."

"Ask yourself, do these numbers appear acceptable to me? Do they make sense? Do you think they reflect how you really feel about each of them?

"Sometimes you might notice a couple of your options have numbers relatively close. I would still weigh each carefully before settling on a definite path. You may notice that some are substantially lower than the others. These shouldn't take any more consideration."

"Goodbye window cleaning." I scratched it off the list.

"I better go help clean up. Do you boys want me to put on another pot of coffee?" She spit in her ashtray, stamped out the half-burned cigarette in the saliva and put it in the breast pocket of her uniform to finish later.

"Yes, thank you."

"I've had enough."

My toes are already feeling like they are dabbling over the edge of an alternative space-time continuum.

	Motorcycle shop	Landscape business	Window cleaning	Video store	College
Freedom 1-15	14	7	6	6	8
Love 1-15	5	5	5	7	10
Meaning 1-15	9	5	3	6	7
Stress -1-15	-12	-10	-8	-6	-14
Insecurity -1-15	-8	-8	-11	-13	-15
Long hours -1-15	-14	-14	-13	-10	-15
Health 1-10	2	8	6	3	4
Free time 1-10	4	4	6	5	3
Value to others 1-10	8	6	7	9	4
Total	8	3	1	7	-8

"What?" The Oracle stared at me.

"Yes, please…" I caved in.

"Let us say that you conclude that running a motorcycle shop is what's right for you. Now you can make another decision-making chart to clarify how your shop should look.

"The possibilities you face now are—rent a building and open a small shop, rent a building and open a big shop, sell new bikes, open a salvage yard, run out of your parent's house until business takes off, or financing and buying an existing shop." He continued to talk as I drew another grid that matched his, with equally crooked lines.

"To customize your list of considerations on the second graph, cut down the quantity of values. Bring it down to your top five or three decisions since you have, mostly, considered them on the first one."

"Sounds fair."

"Instead, consider things directly affecting each option—dealing with employees and customers, mental and financial stress, long term financial reward, equity, and commuting—working out of your parent's garage will most surely come out on top in this category."

"Sure, my mom would love having me around."

"Usually for me, kicking off small will usually win on this list. There is less risk while trying to learn about the market or industry. This is something to consider, especially since you are new to the game.

"You might consider purchasing something already established if you don't want risk, it's an extremely competitive market, or you're not familiar with the industry and would benefit from someone else's help. This way, all that is required of you is to turn on the lights in the morning. But I don't think this applies to you."

"I'm not afraid of a little risk at this stage of my life."

"If this is ever the case, I would be sure that the previous owner includes some type of training before handing over the reins. I've seen a couple of these sales where, as part of the deal, the new owner could observe the operation for a couple of months before the sale was closed."

"Duly noted. It's kind of the same as buying an old fighter jet without asking the former owner how to fly it." I heard a kitchen crew member shut off the radio.

"I think you'll be just fine in this crazy world."

Baby Step #5

"You need a refill?" the Oracle asked me as he returned to the kitchen, where the freshly brewed pot of coffee was still on the burner.

We were the last two in the restaurant. The staff had already put in their dues. Dharma had to go home to her kids and perhaps a drunk husband. It was eerie being here alone by ourselves. Besides being silent, there was almost a hollow sound you could hear when we talked loudly.

They turned the lights down low to save on electricity, but not off, in order for the security cameras to record, and also to scare off thieves—such as potential trucker coffee bandits.

"Sure," I hesitantly replied as I slid my cup to the edge of the table—I knew it was a rhetorical question. "Are you certain it is alright if we're in here?"

"It's not a big deal. Dharma lets me lock up all the time. Besides, what kind of diner closes before midnight? There's not a trucker around the goes to bed that early. It's against the code. In fact, it's downright un-truckerly," he said as he walked back to the table with the whole pot.

"She really has to trust you."

"Character is like a sheet of glass. It sure is easy to see through." He poured my cup before he sat down. "If you possess trustworthiness, people tend to recognize it."

"That must be why everyone calls you the Oracle."

"Which brings us to—number five!"

"Five!" I said with artificial excitement as caffeine propped my brain up.

"This is an important one. It's about goals. Are you awake enough to stay focused?"

"I think I'll be okay as long as I don't blink." My hand trembled ever so slightly as I poured in the creamer.

"Are you as sick as I am from hearing about goals?"

"No, but the night's not over yet."

"If you ever do get tired of it, that definitely means you've been well trained. Since I began being friends with other shoe string entrepreneurs, they've shoved them down my throat. However, this is with good cause.

"I've even attended a few seminars that covered them. In case you haven't had the opportunity of training with a guy sporting a shaved head who is screaming at you, a goal is a written aim you desire to fulfill. It seems simple, but with someone shouting it at you, it seems more significant."

"I hear that. Screaming makes everything seem more important."

"It makes sense, though. If you were driving around the country and got lost, you could pull out a map to figure out where you are. If you have no destination, then the map is useless, and driving around is pointless."

"Pull out a map? You know they have those on your phone now, right?"

"Sure, not the point. Grab your pen. We've got more to do."

"Okay." I slid my cup off the back side of my paper menu, careful not to spill it.

"Write what you would desire to accomplish or gain. Put a timeline of when you would like to reach them. Some might be to open a restaurant, get in shape, run a marathon, or such."

"Is this separate from what we covered in our first chart?"

"You may include items from that. Also, if you really are thinking about opening a motorcycle shop, here's a great place to put it down." He grabbed the pot to refill his cup again, which was surprising because I didn't even notice him drink the last one.

The faster I wrote, the worse my penmanship looked.

"Okay, let me look at your list," he asked. Steam rolled over the brim of the fresh cup of coffee as he took a chug.

"Hopefully my handwriting is readable. It's hard to write with my little pen, not to mention the coffee jitters," I said, sliding it to him.

"Obviously." He leaned his head back as if it would help focus his vision. "First, I must point out here that you wrote, *be a nicer person to others*. That is more of a New Year's resolution.

"A goal has to be measurable and attainable. You could say, *be nice eighty percent of the time*. Then, if you had a Nice-o-Meter, you could calculate how often you were actually pleasant to be around. The Nice-o-Meter is the next invention I will invent, right after I finish making the Idiot-o-Meter."

"Ha!" I faked because I didn't know how to take his humor or if it was in fact meant to be funny.

"I see buying a new car is on your list. I believe that is truly pathetic. You should have goals that are strong and that you feel passionately about."

"Ouch," I mumbled.

"It's also too easy to attain. There are millions of bankers who will lend you money to buy one, even if you can't afford it. I bet the banks generate more profit off of those who miss their payments versus those who are punctual. They earn thousands off of them before they repossess it. Then they will sell it to make up the difference."

"You sound bitter."

"I've seen it too much. The new smell will fade, you will notice more scratches, tires will go bald, it will rust and decay back into the earth they forged it from. All of this solely to fill your insecurities—for what, exactly, was the sacrifice made?"

"To impress girls?"

"Ha! You make me laugh sometimes."

"I'm serious. How do you impress girls without a sweet ride?"

"There are better ways, ways that you won't need to trade your soul for. Let's look at Henry David Thoreau's idea of the true cost of an item being the amount of life which is exchanged for it.

"If you earned twelve dollars an hour and the sports car you yearn for costs sixty-five grand, you would be required to exchange 5,416 hours of your life to pay for it. That's only if you paid with cash in full. If you financed it, you can add significantly more time than that.

"If you worked forty hours a week, had no other expenses but the vehicle, and paid cash for it, you would have no choice but to labor away one hundred and thirty-five weeks to save that much money. That is over two years!

"It is one hundred and thirty-five weekends you wouldn't have time to go camping or fishing with your buddies. How about renting one for a weekend and take a road trip with her instead?"

"You're right. Surely there must be other ways to woo a girl. Perhaps five thousand hours would give me enough time to work on my personality."

"I'm not saying that pursuits like this are pathetic to all people, just nearly everyone. There are individuals who might want it for very passionate reasons. Their father might've really desired one, but couldn't afford it because he was raising a family, and they sincerely wanted to give back for all of his sacrifice."

"That sounds reasonable."

"For everybody else, they need to admit that they want it because they have low self-confidence and insecurity issues that they feel it will fix."

"That's a good point. I'll reword it to say... Buy my dad a new car."

"Starting a motorcycle shop is listed, but nothing else relating to the rest of your life?"

"I'm unable to come up with anything else I might do that far down the road. I know I have my college degree, but I don't know what specific field I'm going to spend my life in. Bikes are my area of expertise. It could be that I'm just choosing something I'm comfortable with for now." I looked out across the empty restaurant, bringing myself back into what an odd moment this was.

"This brings up a good point. I think most individuals set their aspirations too low because they have weak business self-confidence and don't believe that they belong in that world.

"While heading off to their jobs at the tire and lube, they look at tall glass buildings and wish to work in one someday. It is the same mentality of wanting what you can't have.

"They regard the people who are employed there as superheroes and believe that if they were able to get a job there, then they would be somebody."

"Are you saying that if I become a mechanic, that I'm a nobody?" I quickly broke myself from admiring the restaurant and looked over at him.

"You are a somebody if you're doing what you love, regardless of what others think. If you are passionate about bikes, then you are somebody. Never undertake something merely because you believe others will think more or less of you. Are you going to let those idiots rule on what makes you happy?"

"Fair enough."

"I'm just saying, can you work in a glass building? Sure! Can you manage a team of associates? It's feasible. Can you be the lead singer in a rock band? Why not? Can you be a millionaire? Probably, as long as you have greater than a fifth-grade education."

"Some college certainly doesn't hurt, though," I said.

"Some of the most influential people in history dropped out of school. Albert Einstein dropped out of elementary school until he had to return because he flunked the entrance exam at a university. Abraham Lincoln had less than a year of formal education. Unless you have an incapacity directly related to your mission, then it is possible. If it's possible, then what's stopping you from doing it?"

"I still live with my parents," I said so softly that I was doubtful he heard.

"Superstars, musicians, entrepreneurs, and millionaires are not gods—they are people who put their pants on one leg at a time, same as you. At one time, they lived with their parents, too."

"Then how do you start off with nothing?" I spoke in a more audible tone.

"Understand that, whatever the ambition, it will have a cost attached to it. The greater the target, the greater the sacrifice will be. But don't let that stop you from setting off on the journey.

"Do you want to be a millionaire? What would it take? Do you want to sing in a band? How much practice would you need to do? Want to run a marathon? How much would you need to train?

"Passion is the fuel that the unconscious uses to drive you to your goals. Find what makes you tick and it will surprise you with the perseverance you attain."

"I don't know if this is the coffee talking, but I'm ready to roar!"

"Hold up, let's go over your list again." He pushed the menu back to me. "For each goal, ask yourself—why do I want to achieve it? Am I passionate about it? Does achieving this objective fit with my values? What will I be required to do in order to achieve it? How many hours of my life will I need to exchange towards fulfilling it? Do I feel that, in the end, the success will be worth the sacrifice?"

"This is a great deal to take in for one day. I already feel more empowered."

"Well, buckle up. We've got a lot more miles to drive."

The Oracle's Golden Step

Chapter

Five

Like a wet dog, the Beast did one last shake before coming to a rest for the night. So it wasn't parked on the street, the Oracle pulled around to the back of the hotel. With the sounds of the motor and the air brakes, I wondered how many of its patrons we disturbed at two AM.

The establishment was a little dated, but I had no right to complain, since I had no money to contribute to the night's accommodations. Besides that, it would be cool to spend the night in an authentic Route 66 hotel.

Between the sudden silence and sitting in the Beast that late at night, suddenly reality poked through the surreal ambience of the dimly lit alley.

What am I doing? A few days ago, I was a kid living in the room he grew up in and now I'm sitting in a semi-truck in the middle of Arizona with a traveling guru...

"There's something I need to show you," he said as he reached up and turned on the dome light.

"Yes?"

He leaned back and pulled out a large atlas and handed it to me. The cover was missing and all the pages were curled at the edges. It was so old that I wondered how many of the roads have changed by now.

"You really do own a road map!" I sounded similar to an eighth grader teasing his friend because they wore overalls for school that day.

"I know that I can find directions on my phone, but this is my preferred method. This tattered up clump of papers and I have been through a lot. It's not often I require it anymore, but when I do, it is always there."

"Okay—do we need to look up where we're going tomorrow?"
Why are we looking at a map in the dead of the night?

"No, I've driven this route many times now. Reason I'm showing you this is because—number nine!"

"Nine!" I said, trying to return the excitement, but failed to do so because my brown sunshine was wearing off.

"By writing your goals on paper," he began, "your unconscious can form an inner map for you to move toward your desired destination."

"My map?"

"Yes, you won't be aware of it, but it will guide, and sometimes control, every decision you make. Bizarre windows of opportunity could present themselves if you keep your eyes open for them.

"Be warned, however. Not all of these opportunities are beneficial. Your unconscious might not be clear on what the end goal is and it may form its own conclusions."

"How do I get clearer, then?"

"To ward off these distractions, describe every goal on paper clearly and in depth. If you wish for a new bicycle, then describe it in every detail—what color, what brand, what type of tires, and so on. You might end up with a pink tricycle otherwise."

"Pink tricycle?" I asked.

"If you plan on starting a business, then cover every detail. Include how many employees it would require and how much money it nets. If you merely wrote, *I want to own my own business*, you might end up running a hot dog stand in Alaska. Be descriptive, specific, and detailed. Be sure not to leave any holes that must be filled."

"Hot dog stand in Alaska? I actually like that idea."

"Also, try to write all of your objectives in the positive tense. Avoid saying what you don't want, such as, *I don't want to be out of shape* or *I don't want to be poor*. Your inner brain interprets it as you want to be out of shape and poor.

"In goals, two negatives won't make a positive. Instead, form it positive-positive as in, *I want to be in shape* or *I want financial abundance.*

"I could spend the entire night on why your innermost thoughts twist the meaning of double negatives and attracts the opposite of what you desire. However, it would be a lot easier if you simply looked over everything to avoid this trap."

"That sounds reasonable."

"Watch for deceptive words that appear to hold a positively charged meaning, such as, *I want to lose weight* or *I want to quit smoking*. To the subliminal mind, losing things is bad, and it helps you find what's lost. Quitting is also negative—so it could help you start again."

"This seems strange. I'll have to think about it."

"It is unusual, but not only does this make your plans more powerful, it also applies in many areas of life. By writing your objectives, learning the simple language rules, and putting yourself in alignment with your unconscious mind—amazing things tend to happen on your way to success."

"That almost sounds metaphysical."

"Does it? It doesn't have to be. Your consciousness alone is strong enough that it can appear mystical."

"In the morning, I'll take some time to review my goals, write them in more depth, check for negative words or double negatives and rewrite them as positive—if you think it helps."

"I do—and that wraps up the last lesson of the day. We ought to get some shut eye because there's a lot of driving to do tomorrow."

"Okay." I reached over and opened up my door.

"Where are you heading?" he asked.

"Aren't we getting a room?"

"Ha! If we stayed in a hotel everywhere we traveled, we would lose money."

"Then where are we going to sleep? Even if your truck had a sleeper cab, I don't see the possibility of it having bunk beds?"

"We sleep sitting up."

"What?"

"We sleep sitting in our chairs. If they are good enough for us during the day, why are they not good enough for us at night?"

"I never considered that."

"If you feel you're going to fall over, you can always leave your seatbelt on," he laughed.

"Haha…"

"Besides—if you ever intend on getting an office job, you'll have to learn how to sleep in your chair."

Baby Step #7

"Ugh!" the Oracle grunted, waking me from the meager slumber that I fought so hard to achieve. There was barely enough light with the sun coming up that I could look over and notice he was missing.

What is going on?

"Ugh!"

The only thing feasible was that he was dragged from the Beast and was being mugged by what must've been a large group of bandits.

I leaned over and tried to lock my door quietly. Small actions define who we are, but considering there were enough of them to overtake the Oracle, I'll live with that label.

"Ugh! Ninety-two!" he grunted once more.

What is ninety-two? Is it some kind of code? Does he mean 911?

"Ugh! Ninety-three!"

Wait—what?

"Ugh! Ninety-four!"

"What the?" I said out loud as I reached over and opened my door. I walked around the front to catch him doing push-ups on the hard asphalt. "What are you doing?"

"Ugh! Ninety-five… Ninety-six… Ninety-seven… Ninety-eight… Ninety-nine… And one-hundred." He flipped over and sat with his legs crossed. "Push-ups. What does it look like I'm doing?"

"Why are you doing push-ups at the crack of dawn?"

"Many people may not consider this, but the chances your business succeeds has a lot to do with how well your health is. Often, especially in the beginning, you'll be the sole person working toward your achievements. If you don't possess the vigor to attain them and the stamina to stay on course, then your ambitions will come to a rapid halt."

"And that means push-ups at dawn?"

"Truckers never rest—in fact, for every goal on your list, you must make sure that there is a fitness goal adequate to achieve it. I consider that almost all fitness challenges are worth the effort. It allows you to see your objectives all the way to the end."

"That is something I would've never contemplated. You see so many entrepreneurs that are out of shape."

"There are many ways to create success, but you shouldn't limit yourself to these ways."

"You're probably right on that."

"Oh, I almost forgot…"

"What's that?"

"Number seven!"

"Seven!" I faked as the adrenaline was wearing off.

"Seven—stay in shape."

"Simple, but to the point."

Baby Step #8

With the motor compartment being located directly under our seats, it moaned and creaked as though it was a pressure cooker attempting to hold back a nuclear fission reaction.

All the struggle to go barely faster than a person jogging, or to be more descriptive, a middle-aged man trying to keep up running alongside his twenty-five-year-old secretary he regrets leaving his wife and two kids for—thinking he should've stuck with buying a red sports car to fulfill his midlife crisis, but it's too late now.

"Do you want a baloney sandwich?" the Oracle asked me as he held the steering wheel steady with his left knee while spreading mayonnaise on some bread.

"No, thank you," I said, trying to be polite even though I really craved one. "How do you stay so cool driving up the hill this slowly?"

"I could say something fancy, such as you should appreciate the journey and let go of the time you arrive at your destination, but I would say it's more like I enjoy the time to sit back and enjoy my baloney sandwich."

"Still, you have to admit that this is a weakness that America has."

"I don't understand?" he said while chewing on his sandwich.

"Well, in America, we'd rather pave a road up a ninety percent grade than punch a hole in the side of a mountain and make a tunnel. In Europe, we would be driving sixty-eight miles per hour as the relaxing glow of the neon lights flickered as we drove by."

"Maybe this road was made before tunnels became a fad? Or maybe as Americans we prefer to watch the trees go by slowly compared to driving through a concrete tube. Besides, this climb isn't that bad."

"How can you say that?"

"There are two sides to every mountain and for this mountain in particular, the other side is much worse. Coming up that direction is an ascent so vicious they call it head gasket hill because of how many motors blow their head gaskets from overheating."

"Really?"

"I guess it is all about perspective." He bit into his sandwich as if he was a five-year-old diving face first into a birthday cake. I've never seen a man enjoy baloney so much.

"Still, how do you stay so patient while cars fly by honking their horns?"

"If someone gives you a gift, and you refuse to take it, then who does it belong to?"

"The gift giver, I suppose."

"Therefore, if someone gives you their anger and you refuse to accept it, who does it belong to?"

"Them—I suppose."

"Precisely." With every bite more mayonnaise stuck to his mustache.

"Is that lesson supposed to be one of the Baby Steps?"

"No, I would hope that this is common knowledge."

"It appears to be a type of Buddhist philosophy?"

"It might be. I'm not sure where I heard it from, but it really helps to keep a calm demeanor. However, speaking of the Baby Steps," he took another bite out of the sandwich and muffled, "number eight!"

"Eight!"

"Ima..." he paused to swallow. "Excuse me, the bread is a little dry—imagine you are a trucker and for years you've dreamed of driving up this major mountain, a mountain so steep that no semi has ever made it to the top.

"You drove many big hills, trained, and practiced. You know it may demand a sacrifice like you've never dreamed of before, but all you aspire for is to be on top of this mountain, looking out at the infinite miles of scenery."

"Strange metaphor, but I'll follow."

"Now, imagine that you did it. You worked through the suffering, flat tires, broken u-joints, and blown head gaskets. As you look out, you think, is this all there is? I did all that for this?

"Or, even worse—you look out, see another mountain, and think that it was the one that you really should've driven up. Perhaps while you were sitting on top of it, you realized you were more of a sea person. You feel empty inside—as if the sacrifice was for nothing."

"That's depressing." I looked out the window at the trees going by and then back over at him.

"Now, imagine this was your career. How would you feel if you climbed all the way to the top of your profession—only to realize that it isn't what you wanted?

"Like I said before, it usually takes five to seven years before your business is stable and profitable. To be competitive, it would require around seven to ten years.

"You finally reach the peak after ten years of hard labor, struggle, and sacrifice. A decade of your life, of your youth— gone. Every hour you worked is one hour of life you missed. And for what? A new car? A bigger house? Paper money that was made of recycled toilet paper?"

"Even more depressing…"

"Not to worry, though—that primal-reptilian brain of yours can help you out. You could intentionally decide to take a certain road in life, but if your hidden thoughts disagree with your decision, it'll battle you every step of the way.

"Perhaps it forces you to make self-destructive decisions that lead you down the most difficult route. It might sabotage your travel with potholes, speed bumps to climb over, and other obstacles. Is it imaginable that it is the root of bad days, stress, anger, and most of your sacrifice and hard times?"

"Can't I consciously fight these obstacles and challenges?"

"You can fight your inner mind by conscious willpower, but it is merely three percent of your mental capabilities—the other ninety-seven percent is your unconscious.

"It would be the same as trying to beat up a bigger, older brother—a really, really big older brother. People do it all the time. They fight and claw their way to the top, but wouldn't it be much easier to cooperate with this reptilian mind instead of against it?"

"I suppose?"

"There are three major reasons the unconscious sabotages your journey and makes you feel as if a gang of angry monkeys have beaten you—"

"Angry monkeys?"

"—yes, angry monkeys. The reasons could be a loser mentality, low self-confidence, or taking the wrong direction, among other things."

"Like how?"

"First, you must possess certain qualities and attributes to your character in order to be that person who is Mr. or Mrs. successful. There is a difference in how a successful individual acts and behaves versus the loser mentality.

"You must be confident, quick to make decisions, intelligent, knowledgeable about your profession, exhibit good habits, and so forth. Once you present a goal to it—it may think it has a lot of work to do to mold you into this person. Therefore, it may put an obstacle out there for you to grow from."

"Huh?" I really regretted saying no to that sandwich. My breakfast toast and jelly was quickly wearing off.

"This brings us to the second reason it sabotages your journey—self-confidence. If you are filled with pessimistic thinking, or suffer from low self-esteem, your deep mind simply follows the orders."

"I could see a low self-confidence affecting my dating life, but I can't see what it has to do with my professional one?"

"If you think you can't do it, then you probably won't be able to. The unconscious finds ways to make it so. Also, if you go into a deal and lack the faith for it to succeed, or that those deals only materialize for other people, or any other form of pessimistic thinking, then this reptilian brain annihilates any possibility of it happening. Following orders is its job, and it takes every command literally."

Eek—if this is true, I'm doomed.

"How do I get past that?"

"To battle this form of sabotage, a new kind of optimistic thinking needs to be incorporated into your daily life. Your mind has about seventy thousand thoughts a day, most of which play over and over like a tape."

"Seventy thousand?"

I wish for seventy thousand sandwiches. That sounds nice.

"Notice what these thoughts are. What are they saying to you? Are they positive or negative? Even the proclaimed optimist may experience a shockingly large number of destructive thoughts every day."

"You say that I think thousands upon thousands of thoughts a day and you expect them to be all positive?"

"No, but when these destructive notions come to mind, try to find a beneficial one to replace it. Of course, you can't sit there and think of that many upbeat thoughts every day. That would be ridiculous.

"By doing this simple exercise of catching a few undesirable ramblings and making them a little brighter, you may notice with time, you have fewer of them repeating in your head. Things will go more smoothly for you in everyday life."

"And this affects my chances of success?"

"Many books have been written on the power of positive thinking. Solely by observing the undesirable thoughts you think—things will change noticeably. We are merely human, though. Even the greatest and most spiritual minds are infected by this elusive darkness. The game is to outweigh them with the optimistic ones."

"That's quite the task."

You hear that glum goblin? I'm coming after you!

"The third reason that the unconscious sabotages you is because you are driving up the wrong mountain and it will do all it can to pull you off from your path before you waste too much of your life trying to conquer it."

"And if I overpower it and succeed anyhow?"

"If by chance you do, it will toil day and night to pull you back down. You hear of people making millions only to lose it all, then make it back, and lose it all again. This is most likely why.

"They may say it was just bad luck, but it would be more accurate to say that they made poor decisions. They put themselves in dangerous positions by being influenced by the unconscious."

"How do you know if it is beating on you to mold you into the person you need to be in order to succeed, or if the beatings are because you are on the wrong path?"

"That's easy," he paused as he threw the last of the sandwich in his mouth and seemingly swallowed it whole, "is the evil troll of emptiness following your every footstep? Do you feel empty most of the time, but it's broken up by spurts of excitement?"

"Evil troll of emptiness?" I muttered.

At least my glum goblin will have someone to be friends with up there.

"If you are driving up the right hill, you may still experience obstacles and bad days. No matter how bad things get, you still hold a passion for it deep down inside. You know nothing can stop you—that quitting is not an option.

"The only thing you can do is keep going because, to you, there are no other hills to climb. Then you'll be working in harmony with your unconscious self.

"It effortlessly guides you down the easiest path and with the least number of challenges. It shows you the quickest way over or around what obstacles there are.

"With passion, you unlock the other ninety-seven percent of your mind and you can find power that you never knew you had. Things will simply flow your way, like standing in a flood zone during a monsoon season."

"Maybe you're right—maybe I am a sea person."

Baby Step #9

"Hey Distributor Dan, is this a good place to drop?" the Oracle asked the man who climbed up on the driver's side steps of the Beast and held onto the mirror after we backed up to the dock.

I'm not sure why I imagined we were dropping it off at a grocery store, even though it was loaded with potatoes.

"Sure, Jimmy Z," the man replied. "Leave it here and I'll deal with it on Monday. We can always use that second bay and we've got the yard dog if we choose to move it."

"I don't understand how a dog can move the trailer?" I asked.

"That kid is funny!" He followed with the same chuckle as the drunk mall Santa had from when I was a child.

"The yard dog is a semi-truck looking vehicle used to move trailers around the yard. It is small, slow, and ugly. Typically, the only time they pass through that gate is when they're brand new and when they get hauled out with the trash pile."

"Oh."

"It's a bit early to be going home, isn't it?" The Oracle looked back over at Distributor Dan.

"The boss won't miss me." They both cackled at the inside joke.

"If you say so." The Oracle chuckled again.

"The carburetor I ordered for my hot rod came in yesterday and I'm itching to go put it on."

"Just remember to run the idle a little rich. That way, it won't be so sensitive to the ignition timing. You know how those old engines go?"

"That's a helpful reminder. I might lose a little horsepower on the bottom end, but it should run a whole lot smoother."

"If you ever decide to race it, let me know. I'll come over and static time it to get it really dialed in."

"I might take you up on that offer. In the meantime, go ahead and unhook. I'm going to take off—just lock the gate behind you," he said as he climbed off the steps and walked away.

"Sounds good." The Oracle hopped out of the Beast and fussed with things around the backside of its cab.

I followed in case he could use some help. "What are you doing?"

"Going to leave the trailer here," he said as he broke the airlines free.

"Are we going to come back after it?"

"Why? This isn't mine."

"It's not? Who is the owner of it, then?"

"I don't know. I simply go where I'm told, pick up the load I'm told to pick up, and drive it to where it needs to go." He started cranking down the landing gear.

"But this is your rig, right?"

"It is."

"Okay, I understand now. So, we're going somewhere else to pick up a different load?"

"Eventually. We're going to bobtail it for a while."

The landing gear began to pull the weight off from the back of the Beast.

"What's a bobtail?"

"It means we won't have a trailer for a little while—until we pick up a skeletal trailer over in California, that is."

"Skeletal? You mean one full of human remains?"

"Ha—" he looked over at me. "No, it's a type of trailer that they attach a shipping container to. But—yeah, I guess it could be full of skeletons. I make it a habit to not open the doors to find out." He reached in through the rear tires and pulled the handle to the kingpin. "There, ready to roll."

"That didn't take long."

"You get fast at hooking and unhooking. Do you know what else will go by real fast?"

"What?"

"Number nine!"

"Nine!"

"But first," he went over and grabbed the King from the floorboard, "you want some coffee?"

"I could use a little." I went over to my side of the Beast and grabbed my travel mug.

When I came back around the front, he was over by the loading dock, using it as a table to fill the cap of his thermos. I climbed the side stairs to the top of the dock, went over and sat next to the King, then kick my legs over the edge.

"Are you going to be okay drinking this coffee black?"

"I'll do fine."

"Learning salesmanship is essential to success," he said as he poured my cup.

I was grateful that there was no steam coming out of it. The day was already hot enough without the added help.

"I wouldn't think that sales have anything to do with truck driving."

"Everything is a sale of some sort. From the time you wake up, you are selling yourself to others. By talking about old cars and carburetors, I sold Distributor Dan on thinking of me the next time he has a load of potatoes needing hauled.

"I sold Snow Queen Sally the benefits of being my friend. I sold Dharma on letting me stay in the diner after they closed so I could squeeze in a few extra cups of coffee. I sold myself on driving today and dropping this load. Everything you do is selling to others—or even selling something to yourself."

"Interesting—go on." I took a large swig of his homemade trucker coffee and, to my surprise, my eyes started watering up.

"When you master the fine art of salesmanship—you hold the power to create affluence, motivate, and inspire."

"That almost sounds like a superpower?" I focused on not blinking.

Tears are not tears until they leave the eye.

"It is, so you should be careful with it. With delicate honesty and abundant product and client knowledge, your superior salesmanship qualities will soon become apparent."

"How does this knowledge apply to truck driving?"

"I know my industry. I know my clients and what they prefer. Often, I know where to drop the load, what times they are available for unloading, and we treat each other as family.

"Keep in mind that your duty is to bring value to others. Make sure your clients get the most out of what they are paying for. Ensure that if you are selling an idea or concept that the other person also reaps the benefits."

"How does selling an idea help others?" I took another massive slug of the black sunshine, knowing dang well that I had to finish the whole cup.

"Would the concept of graduating high school or college benefit your friends? Clearly it would—so constantly sell that notion to them.

"Would having overpriced toilet paper delivered to your front door bring value? It might to some people, but most can just drive after it. Sell to those who exhibit a need and leave the rest alone. They don't want you."

"You're saying not to sell my friends the idea of going to college if it doesn't benefit them?"

"Exactly. In fact, I would say a good rule in sales is to treat everybody as if they were a good friend. You wouldn't sell your friends on something that won't benefit them, would you?"

"Absolutely not." I rubbed my tongue on the outside of my teeth, trying to clear out some rogue coffee grounds that were irritating my gums.

"Then if you sold real estate—would selling your clients a new house be in their best interest? Would it be better if they stayed where they are? Even if it meant losing a commission? Would you ever think to ask why they are moving?

"If they are moving because they are unhappy with their lives, not their house, will they benefit from a different house but the same lives? If you sell them a new house and they don't benefit from it, you are not creating value for them."

"I hope I never sell myself on selling real estate. That's a cruel profession."

"Regardless of the type of business, strive for your past clients to be your best salespeople. Word of mouth advertising is the cheapest and most effective. No other way of advertising creates such dramatic results. The only way to create this form of advertising is by offering a service or product that's worthy of talking about."

"Why didn't you just say to treat everyone like they are your friend?" I held my breath and took three big gulps.

"That's a little over simplified, but yes—that would work too."

Chapter

Six

Baby Step #10

"Take in that smell, Bud," the Oracle said with a deep inhale as he and the King walked in through the door of Sam's Motorcycle Emporium.

"It's great."

It smells like old oil, new gas, and broken bones. I would wear it as a cologne if I could.

Dropping the trailer and driving around bobtail gave us some luxuries we didn't have before. With the trailer, we were limited to mostly interstate highways and truck stops. We could now go easily within the walls of the inner-city of Phoenix.

Rather than feeling we like were driving a small house, it now felt as if we were driving a large RV. Even though we could squeeze into most places, it was still more comfortable parking on the outer edges of large parking lots, or in this case, a mostly empty one.

It was a smaller shop that was dilapidated and if it wasn't for the flickering open sign, I would've assumed they had gone bankrupt and closed up.

Oddly, it was also next-door to what must've been the city's largest motorcycle dealership. You know the kind—nice enough to sell Italian sports cars, if that is what they desired.

"From here, can you tell me what each of these are?" he asked.

Standing near the entrance, there were two rows of about forty used motorcycles, mostly dirt bikes.

"Please, make it a little more challenging. I could tell you the model of every one of them purely by the shape of the rear fender. I could tell you the size of the motor solely by the exhaust pipe."

"Impressive, but I didn't bring you here to test your knowledge of them."

"Then why are we here?"

Please let it be to test ride stuff.

"Because… Number ten!"

"Ten!"

"You have written your goals thoroughly and feel good about them, so the next step is to make them reality. If your goal is to buy a new house on a hill—then imagine your car in the driveway in front of the garage, walking up the white sidewalk, past the grass which is sprouting, turning the new doorknob and pushing the smoothly moving white door open.

"You take your shoes off at the door, walk barefoot across the brand-new carpet into a kitchen with freshly stained wood cabinets and a counter that shines. All the appliances and windows still have the labels on them from the factory. The entire house smells of new carpet and fresh paint. Everything shines and looks fresh out of the box."

Obviously, I'll have to buy new furniture, too.

"That sounds nice."

"You walk through the master bedroom and into the master bathroom, which is bigger than the living room in your current house. You notice the nice, new, triangle-shaped jet tub in the corner. From the back of the master bedroom, there is a raised deck with a hot tub that looks over the valley."

"What does visiting this joint have to do with buying a new house?"

"Your conscious mind may know better than to think this is real, but your unconscious mind has no clue. It takes everything imagined and sets into motion swift action to make it happen, as if it was a concrete reality. The amount of passion for the idea determines the energy the unconscious puts toward its fulfillment."

"You're saying that before I pursue a goal, I should daydream about it first?"

Finally, an exercise I can get behind.

"Or even better, set aside some time as soon as possible to take the first baby step towards your goal. If your goal is to buy that house, then drive around and look at houses. Go to an open house or call the realtor to see inside the one you want.

"While you're in there, touch everything. Don't be afraid of looking strange and doing what you need to do in order to imagine that you are already the owner."

"And that'll increase the chances of success?"

"The more you can make it a reality in your head, the more likely it becomes a reality in your outer world. Go as far as making an appointment with a mortgage lender and asking them how much money you would have to earn in order to buy this house, and what kind of debt-to-income ratio you would need. Then make a plan to pay off your debt and save money."

"Which brings us here?"

"Yes, if you wanted to open up something resembling this place, look up all the similar ones in the phone book. Take a drive around your town, observe and count all of them. Drive around various neighborhoods and try to estimate how many people there are per shop. Notice how busy they are. Do you see a need for one somewhere? Is the parking lot empty?

"Walk inside these places and look around. Take in the smells. Touch the bikes. Notice the new parts for sale on the walls. Drag your feet across the floor. Can you see yourself running a place the same as this?"

"I see your point."

I suddenly have the urge to take my shoes off and run my stockinged feet across the worn oil-stained carpet, but fear ruining my socks.

Baby Step #11

"Security is a little low around here," I mentioned.

"Why do you say that?" The Oracle looked around.

"We've been walking around for about 20 minutes looking over all these motorcycles and haven't seen a single employee."

"Often the guy running the counter is also the mechanic with these smaller operations."

"I would think that a shop this size would have more than one employee, though."

"That's a good point, but it gives us more time."

"More time for what?"

"Number eleven!"

"Eleven!"

"At the root of business is the same core concept as the ancient marketplace. You are trying to exchange something of value for something else of value. In order to be successful at it, you need to find ways to bring value to others.

"You offer value through physical labor such as repairing broken crap, intellectual labor such as being an accountant, or making a product accessible to a consumer, such as this wall covered in sprockets and handlebars for sale."

"Sounds basic, but I'll follow."

"It is, but you're probably making things too complicated. Sometimes we need to simplify things and go back to the basics. To attain money, you must simply create value for someone else—that's it."

"Still following." I straddled one of the few street motorcycles and tilted it to an upright position, holding the handlebars as if I was riding it.

It was a chopper, which meant it had long front forks causing the front wheel to be a few feet out in front of its main body. The fuel tank had flames painted down the side of it and the rest of it was all chrome. It had ape hanger handlebars, which, as the name may describe, were tall, which caused my arms to dangle from them.

"The synonym for money is hard physical labor or thought. The harder you think, the less you need to work physically. Focus on the needs of others and express your talents to fulfill those needs.

"In return, this draws affluence to you. The question you should ask yourself is, 'Am I really being of great value? Am I worth the money I receive for my efforts? If someone else offered the services to me, would I be willing to pay them?'"

"Umm…" I watched the cars out front pass by as I dreamed of being among them on this chopper, cruising the open road, living life to the fullest.

"If you worked forty hours a week, fifty weeks a year from the time you turned eighteen until you turned sixty-five, you would have only spent less than fourteen percent of your life at work. This is assuming that you live until you're eighty years old.

"Do you feel that what you do to create value is worthy enough to pay for the other eighty-six percent of your life? Are you worth what you get paid for each hour of your life that's exchanged for money?

"You not only need to be worth the one hour of life you exchange for one hour of pay—you need to be six times that. That one hour at work needs to pay for over six hours away from it. This is only to support you."

"If you're a single-family income house, and raising children, the value you create for others had better be worth gold. And this doesn't include earning enough money to buy a sweet ride like that to go riding with your buddies on the weekends."

"This may be a ridiculous question, but how do I create value for others?" I didn't break my focus from looking out the window.

A biker must always keep their focus on the road ahead.

"Analyze what you would desire in your life and ask yourself, would other people also want this? Would they want it enough to exchange hard-earned money for it? Would this be filling a need that isn't currently being filled?

"Market trends show what needs are in demand. Follow these and be adaptable to meet the ever-changing markets. If you can fill these needs, you create value. It's that simple."

"Indeed." I went back to daydreaming of the open road. I would've been making bah, bah, bah motorcycle noises if he had not been standing next to me.

Baby Step #12

"You'd look pretty good riding that down the road," the sales attendant-counter help-mechanic said as he approached us.

"Thanks, but I'm only looking." I quickly flipped out the kickstand and dismounted from the chopper.

So embarrassing!

"Is Sideways Sam here?" the Oracle asked.

"I'm afraid not. I just barely bought this place from him. My friends call me Grease Monkey Gary."

"It's a pleasure to meet you Grease Monkey Gary. I'm Jimmy Z, and this is Bud. What happened to Sideways Sam?"

I could tell that he was more of a motorcycle enthusiast than a salesman by not offering to shake our hands. I was thankful for this. It wasn't because his hands were oil stained, it was because it's awkward. It's not 1952—leave my hand alone.

"Real bad news. Do you know how he was a diabetic?"

"I remember that."

"Well, he was giving himself insulin and hit a vein."

"I wouldn't wish that on my worst enemy. Is he okay?"

"He is now, but he had to close the shop for a few months and never really recovered financially. I stepped in and bought this before the bank could foreclose on it."

"Why did they call him Sideways Sam?" I asked.

"Some people are honest in their dealings and walk forward in a straight line. Some people walk that line a little more crooked than others. Well, he walked sideways, so to speak." The Oracle smiled.

"Oh…"

"Yes, sir." Grease Monkey Gary cleaned his glasses on his shirt, which I suspected only made them dirtier. "People would bring in their rides for a tune-up and he would disconnect the ignition coil.

"When they would come to pick it up, he would say that it had a blown motor and offered them a scrap metal price. When they would check it over and realize that it didn't run at all—they would agree."

"That's horrible."

"When I bought this place and found that out, I had to call all the previous owners and give them their bikes back. Dang near completely wiped out my inventory."

"Why would you be friends with someone like that?" I asked the Oracle.

"Nobody is perfect—it's simply that some people have many, many more faults than others. When you have as many friends as I do, you have to learn to look over their imperfections."

"What if they are true scoundrels? What if they try to take advantage of you?"

"I can say that while you'll be much happier in life when you learn to accept people as they are, regardless of their faults, you must also know what those blemishes are and protect yourself against them.

"If you have a friend that borrows twenty bucks and then doesn't pay you back, then simply never lend them money again and everything should be alright. If your friend is a swindler, then don't do business with them. If they are the type to hit on your girl—then they should never meet her.

"It's not saying that these people are great friends, but I believe everybody has value that they can add to a friendship. Even though I would never, ever, buy anything from him—he could tell a joke that was so dirty that he would even offend himself."

"That's true. I barely knew the guy, but some of them jokes really haunt me."

"Is that the Baby Step I'm supposed to learn?"

"No, it's merely a good way to go about your friendships. Find what value they offer and protect yourself from their shortcomings. But that brings us to—number twelve!"

"Twelve!" I said, returning the loudness and startling our new friend.

"To make money you must create value, so what part of ripping people off like he did to others creates value? By taking advantage of others, you are teaching your brain to think that resources are scarce. Therefore, you need to get your share by taking from others."

"That's why I gave everybody back what belonged to them."

"There is an abundance of wealth, you do not need to get wealthy by stealing from others. You cannot buy peace of mind, nor can you be successful while feeling guilty at the same time.

"If you do not see this abundance of wealth, it might be because you haven't programmed your mind to see opportunities."

"Isn't there some gray area, such as sales? After all, doesn't a sales agent have to be aggressive to make a sale? At what point do they become sleazy?" Grease Monkey Gary asked, as if sales were a new topic in his life. He seemed as the type of guy who felt more comfortable back in the shop than on the showroom floor.

"The difference between persuasion and manipulation is the intent of who will be served. Manipulation is a transaction when one party benefits more than the other—Sideways Sam only thought of himself.

"Persuasion is give and take, finding a mutually agreeable ground where both parties receive value. If you are the only one benefitting, the other parties will take their money elsewhere.

"Likewise, if you give while receiving nothing in return, you will soon be bankrupt. A successful business is run on the principle of a mutual win-win."

"Got it—I'm sure I'll find balance where everybody wins."

"You create value by making those win-win opportunities. You need to provide a service that benefits all parties that are involved—while being fair, reasonable, and treating others with honor and respect. If you can do all this, then you may have customers for life."

"Do you want a job as a sales associate?"

The Oracle chuckled, but I think that he was serious.

Baby Step #13

"Do you mind if I ask you how you acquired this shop?" the Oracle asked.

All three of us now sat on a motorcycle. I was in the center with my chopper. Grease Monkey Gary, to my right, was sitting on a classical mid 70s scrambler with a green and mustard yellow fuel tank.

The Oracle sat on my left on a modified late 60s café style racer with handle bars so short that you would think that they were only a novelty—the King rested over the instrument cluster as if he too was enjoying the imaginary ride.

"Sure—" He leaned forward and whipped the throttle back as if it was running. "—back in junior high, I hung out with the wrong crowd. It's not that they smoked in the boy's room or anything such as that. These boys, well, and one girl, which we nicknamed Adrenaline Junkie Angie, all liked to go fast—very fast.

"We would terrorize our neighborhoods with our rapped-out exhausts and the smell of burnt two-stroke fuel—that is until the cops would show up and make us walk our bikes back home."

I pulled my throttle wide open. I knew we were pretending, but I wanted to keep up.

"That's the thing about these—for one reason or another, you always end up pushing them home." The Oracle twisted his throttle, too.

"I knew that one day I wanted to be the owner of my own shop." He leaned back and cut the throttle to half. Whatever car he must've passed in his mind was far behind him now. "When I heard Sideways Sam needed a quick sale, I drove down to the closest mortgage broker and pulled out a second mortgage on my house. Next thing I knew, I was unlocking the door for my first day of operation."

With a double beep of the old café's horn, the Oracle yelled out, "Number thirteen!"

"Thirteen!" I followed with a single beep from my chopper. For as cool as this thing was, the horn did not emit that coolness. If someone honked it in the dark, you would think an early 80s compact car was trying to pick a fight with you.

"I'm not saying that refinancing your home to start a business is a good idea necessarily." The Oracle looked over at me. "While it is one of the easiest ways to attain funds, since you don't need a business plan to secure the financing—if it fails, you may end up losing your home as well."

"What is a business plan?" I asked.

"Let's start off with the plan of action. Pull out that menu we wrote your goals on."

"Ok," I said as I unfolded it and spread it across the handle bars and fuel tank of the chopper.

"The last part of goal-making is creating a plan of action. I saved mentioning this exercise until we were here. By running around and touching things, such as the bikes in this shop, not only were you making it real in your unconscious, but it also allowed you to be gathering information and data to make a sounder plan of action."

"Plus, who doesn't enjoy visiting shops?" I asked.

"—and hanging out with the owners." Grease Monkey Gary added.

"Especially that—by talking to professionals, you may gain useful information. If you are going to be competition for them, be careful not to annoy them.

"However, if they are the people who are going to make money off of you, such as a banker, mortgage broker or real estate agent—torture them mercilessly with your endless questions."

"I don't mind helping a young biker with what I know."

"We appreciate your input," I shot out some gratitude.

"Yes, thanks again."

"No problem."

"The next part is to write your plan of action in every detail."

"Ok." I started to pull out my sawed-off pen.

"Not now, though. There's so much more we need to cover first."

"Alright." I nonchalantly shoved it back down into my pocket with my thumb.

"Before you start writing, you must realize that the world of the unconscious is ridiculous. It is the conscious mind's job to make things sane. Once the unconscious accepts a goal, it is ruthless in acquiring it.

"This might seem strange, but if you want your future wife and children to join you in your success, include that statement somewhere on the plan of action. You should also include if you want to hold on to your friends and if, after you succeed, people are generally going to like you."

"Seriously?"

"Seriously—your unconscious could and does shed and destroy anything in its path that is in the way of achieving your goal. Be sure to take some time to list all the things and relationships that you have which the unconscious might destroy in its pursuit. Include them in the plan of action and the final-vision."

"Final-vision?"

"We'll get to that later, but be very clear on this exercise, and include everything. Forgot about your boat? Hope it doesn't get in the way."

"Are you psychic?" Grease Monkey Gary suddenly looked over. "I was short on the closing costs and had to sell my boat."

"They do call him the Oracle," I mentioned as if I believed he might actually predict the future.

"The Oracle?"

"Then," he continued on, not acknowledging or denying his abilities to be a soothsayer, "once again, look over each of your goals and plan of action. Eliminate the double negatives and negative words, turning them all into positive statements.

"Instead of saying, *I hope my wife doesn't leave me*, you could say, *All of my family shall reap success and love me. We will be together as a family*."

"Writing goals and a plan of action seems like a tedious task." I folded the menu back up and stuffed it in my back pocket.

"It is, but by spending a few hours clarifying what you want—you build a foundation for your future empire. You create a map to follow and make an instruction manual for dealing with obstacles."

"Whoa, metaphor overload."

"Well, in a sense, you allow yourself a level of autopilot where you go through the motions set out and success naturally floats your way."

"Better—why didn't you just say it that way to begin with?"

"There are not enough ways to say it that implies it strong enough. Goals and a plan of action are the key to unlocking the unconscious mind. The unconscious mind is powerful—it is your aim to be in harmony with this grand force."

"A psychic and a poet?" Grease Monkey Gary smiled.

"Ha! Which finally brings us to what a business plan is." The Oracle turned his focus to looking back at the window. He lifted both feet onto the foot pegs as if he was riding, though it was sitting still, and somehow miraculously kept his balance.

"Great!"

"It is basically a plan of action with a bunch of numbers. It requires a ton of research, the more the better, and calculations on how you predict your venture will operate and how much money it should make. Although, ultimately, these numbers are nothing more than an educated guess."

"A guess?" I stuttered a little.

"Sounds right. I bought this place on basically a sophisticated hunch."

"That is why so much research is required. The more information you can gather, the more probable it is that these numbers will be somewhat accurate. For getting a loan, they would prefer to see numbers accurate enough that even though they too know it's an estimate, they at least need to make sense of them."

"—and I skipped that total nightmare by refinancing my house. Risky? Yes, but simple. I did, however, still create a detailed plan for my sake. Even though the numbers may not be exactly what I can expect, I have a guide I can use and when I'm not on course, I can adjust, possibly advertise or have a sale."

"You see, despite business plans not being as accurate as we would hope, they have purpose. With enough research, you won't need a crystal ball to see your chances of success—it'll be all in the numbers."

Baby Step #14

"Vrrrooom!" a muffled noise emitted from inside the street helmet of Grease Monkey Gary.

His eyes fixed straight ahead as if some eminent danger awaited. Maybe a car will dash out in front, maybe it will be a child running out into the street, maybe, just maybe, there might be gravel on the road. *Eeek!*

But none of those were the case. In fact, I'm not sure why he was wearing a helmet. The three of us remained sitting stationary on our respective motorcycles on the tattered showroom floor.

"What?" I asked.

"Oh, nothing," he said as he flipped the visor open so we could hear him clearly. "Safety is important. So much so that you'll almost never see me near one of these without the proper safety gear."

"That's strange. I thought bikers were all about living on the edge."

"The only ones who say that are those who don't know where the edge is. They think a casual stroll down the road is the brink of danger and, yes, luck might be on their side and this trip won't be the one they need the helmet—though I assure you someday they will.

"Until they take corners so fast that the sidewalls of their tires heat up and turn blue—then they have no clue what the edge looks like. That edge needs safety equipment."

"Number fourteen!" the Oracle interrupted us.

"Fourteen!" I responded.

"He touched on a very important aspect to consider before setting out to become an entrepreneur—safety. The safest path is to buy something that already exists. You can see the established income before you invest. That, however, is also why they are expensive to buy. Someone took all the risk of starting it."

"Very true," Grease Monkey Gary chimed in.

"That is how Sideways Sam created value—despite being sideways. When he signed the lease for this building, he committed himself to months or even years of payments. He spent thousands on tools. He paid thousands on inventory he didn't know for sure would sell. Not knowing if a single customer would show, he put all of his saved up, hard-earned money on the line.

"This is what Grease Monkey Gary paid for when he signed the dotted line—a business with the bulk of the risk reduced."

"It's still dangerous. Anything can happen. But, yes, same as taking a bike for a test ride before purchasing it, it's nice to see if an operation is a well-oiled machine before risking your investment."

"That makes a good point," the Oracle said, "would you rather buy a motorcycle that came torn down into tiny pieces by some teenager and stored in a box with the possibility that the pieces might not fit, some might be missing, or any other of the infinite possibilities making sure that it never runs again—or would you rather buy one already running?

"One you can ride down the street listening to the smooth rumble of a perfectly tuned motor? That, in essence, is what Sideways Sam did. He put the place together and made it hum."

"What about for those who don't have a house to refinance or a small fortune to invest? What about the people like me with hardly enough to start? Is there no hope?" I asked.

"There is," he rested his hands on the fuel tank, "there is…"

Chapter

Seven

Baby Step #15

And with the slow *whir-whir-whir*, the motor coughed once and went silent. Grease Monkey Gary pushed in the starter button once more only to get a click-click-click. The battery was dead. The entire showroom smelt like fuel from the flooded motor.

"I'm sorry. I work hard for my money and I will not spend it on junk," the customer with his, what one could assume to be stepchild he was trying to impress, said as if he was on a different pedestal.

"This ran well when I parked it, but they don't like to sit for very long. They tend to get fussy. This is a good one for the money. The problem is that you don't have enough of it. You come in here and say that you only have enough money for my cheapest bike and yet you expect it to run like brand-new.

"For your information, not even brand-new motorcycles run like brand-new. There is no such thing as a reliable motorcycle— only ones that try to fool us into believing they are.

"My recommendation is to go next door, finance a new one so you can afford it, and enjoy the first year that it may or may not run well." He nearly forcefully ushered them out the door.

"Well, I never!" the rejected customer said as if he was a 1880s princess being insulted by a commoner.

He slid a brick in front of the door to keep it open, to let the gas fumes out, walked back to his scrambler he was sitting on next to me, put his helmet back on, closed the visor, and yelled.

"Does that happen often?" I asked.

"What? The bike's not starting or a popper pretending to be a prince?" He lifted his visor back up.

"Both—I guess?"

"For both, I'd say much too often. You see, people have the wrong idea of these machines. They think because the motors are smaller, then they should be more reliable. The opposite is true, actually. The bigger they are, the better they run.

"Look at diesel semi-truck engines compared to gasoline car motors. Jimmy Z—how often does your engine leave you stranded on the side of the highway?"

"Almost never."

"And how many miles does it have?"

"Slightly over two million. A good diesel doesn't get broken in until the odometer hits seven digits. It's still in its prime."

"Yet a car motor will be lucky to see a tenth of that and bikes, a tenth of a car. Most only make it to twenty thousand miles, and start becoming unreliable at around fifty miles.

"One of the many problems is that it has the same number of parts of the larger motors, but in much, much smaller size. It's no wonder they are always hard starting and needing maintenance."

"Would it be of value if, say, some neighborhood kid came by every morning to make sure everything sitting on the showroom floor started effortlessly?" the Oracle asked.

"That would be of great value indeed."

"Then I only have one thing to say."

"What's that?" I asked.

"Number fifteen!"

"Fifteen!" This time Grease Monkey Gary joined in.

"Completely the same as starting up a stubborn, complex motorcycle—starting a business has many minute components that must all work in perfect harmony in order for it to survive.

"Same as the neighborhood kid coming by every morning and starting each of these adds value, so does the person who starts the business and gets it running smoothly for the next guy."

"You mean the same as what Sideways Sam did with this joint?"

"Yes, but there are people out there whose sole intent is to start up a business, run it for a few years, and then sell it as a stable enterprise. They are the ones that absorb all the initial risks, the struggles that come with starting it, and the stress of not knowing if it was going to make it another day. This is extremely risky, but highly profitable. To say the least—it is not something an amateur would want to take on."

"I cannot imagine living my life that way. The constant stress—nope, not for me."

"That seems like a rough way to live a life," I said.

"You're both right. I believe these people must be into self-torture. Regardless, I mention this because this is one more way that people make money by creating value for others."

Baby Step #16:

"Excuse me—do any of you work here?" the young man, who looked like he was freshly retired from his teen years, asked.

"That's me!" Grease Monkey Gary looked over and flipped the visor of his helmet open.

"Do you have any two-stroke oil?"

"I do…" He unstrapped his helmet and rested it on top of the mirror of the scrambler.

Everyone knows that the only useful thing about a motorcycle side mirror is to hold your helmet. When using it while riding down the road, all you can typically see in it is the world behind you shaking violently back and forth.

After he left to help his customer, the Oracle and I continued to sit on our retro sleds while looking out of the window.

Not to stereotype motorcyclists, but yes, we tend to fit in a certain category—especially those who ride dirt bikes. There are three typical different types of young adults who ride them.

The first type are young women. They ride because they are cool. I'm sure there are more reasons than that, but to me, there's nothing more attractive than a young lady in a riding jersey.

The second type, which I hope is a category that I am in, is young men who enjoy it for the spiritual side, the thrill of the ground rushing underneath them, and the timelessness of floating through the air. There is no other experience like it on earth.

The third type are young men, which by no fault of their own, were simply born ugly. Don't feel bad for this youth as they are most likely to be the fastest kid on the track. They approach everything full throttle, they clear every triple, and have more trophies than the local high school football star.

By the looks of this kid—he was really fast.

"Number sixteen!" the Oracle shouted, catching me off guard.

"Sixteen!" I returned the excitement and brought my focus back to why we were here.

"If you don't have the money to buy an existing operation, then there are certain things you must know in order to reduce the risk. You wouldn't buy a brand-new motorcycle without first researching it—would you?"

"Of course not."

"In the same manner, you shouldn't do anything new without a considerable amount of research—call it your due diligence."

"Do you mean how to run it?"

"Well, yes, but more than that, how you fit into this world. Remember, it is your job to create value for others. If that particular value was already being filled—are you really adding more?"

"I guess not."

"Demographics track the density of businesses relative to the population. They are all the facts that decipher what needs

are being met by the current establishments and what needs still have to be met. The concept is very simple—find out what they are doing and do it in a different market. Find a hole in the market and model the success of others.

"If you live in a small town with no automotive junk yard and that's what you want to do, then collect a ton of data from your desired market and compare it to a similar one. Figure out what they do to be successful and do it in your town."

"What should I consider as a similar market?"

"Let us say that you want to open a coffee shack. Your market is a suburban area of Salt Lake City. You want to collect data from all the places in your competitive market—then you want to find a non-competitive one to compare with your area. You want the markets to be as similar as possible. In other words, you want to compare apples to apples."

"How do I do that without having access to that data?"

"If you did want to open a coffee shack, decide on an area across town with roughly the same population and income level. You notice that there are three shacks in a five-mile radius in your area, and five within a five-mile radius in your comparable market.

"If, inside your comparable market, the five shacks are all profitable—then do you think it's possible for a fourth one in your area to make money?"

"And what if there were the same number, or more, of them in my area?"

"If there were five shacks in your area and three in your comparable market, then consider things before you open a sixth. Then again, if there are five in your area and they are all profitable, you may still want to consider opening another.

"Or, with your new data, you may want to open one in your comparable market. The more information you collect, the more options you create. This means that you can better predict the outcome of your efforts. This is called analyzing demographics."

"What if something in my related market closed down?"

"Realize that an old business will fall to the ground and another will be built on top of its ashes. Simply because one closes down doesn't mean that it wasn't profitable.

"I've seen them go down because of—losing the lease on their building, losing a distributor, the owners lost interest in it, the owners moved, violations shut it down, the owners' health problems interfered, or my favorite—the old owners were incompetent idiots. The last one is most often the case, I've noticed.

"Research is the key to succeeding on the ashes of others. Find out exactly why they failed and why you won't. Be thorough with your demographics. Don't make the same mistakes they did—or the outcome will also be the same.

"Snow Queen Sally's had outstanding success from the failure of others. The failures didn't occur because there weren't enough customers—it was merely that, after a couple of years of waking up at two in the morning and working in the cold, many plow drivers became tired and quit."

"She is one tough lady."

"She is—she makes thousands every time it snows and is still turning away accounts. Whenever she stops for a cup of coffee, she ends up plowing that locations lot. People flag her down in the road to get her to plow their entrances so they can open for the day. All of this began only weeks after she bought her first plow truck."

"Who would have thought it—with all the plow trucks you see out there, that there would be any available customers left?"

"Fortunately, she found a hole in the market big enough to drive a truck through."

"That's a good way to say it."

"There are millions of successful people out there that won't be where they're at in years to come. Society will need successors to fill their roles. This can be you or somebody else—it's your choice.

"Rock bands break up, entrepreneurs retire or go broke, sometimes people simply quit and there is a hole where they stood. For every band that breaks up, one more needs to come along and take their place—that could be you. For every entrepreneur that retires, someone else needs to pick up the demand left in the market—that could be you. For every person who quits—you can take over and succeed.

"Currency flows like the currents of the river that carry water from one lake to another. Old lakes will dry up and new lakes will form where there used to be none. Oceans and millionaires are not exempt from this fact of life. The outflow cannot be stopped—as soon as the intake slows, the lake will run dry. The old will pass their wealth to the young—eventually."

"Wow…" I went back to gazing out the window.

That could be me!

Baby Step #17

"Thanks for letting me borrow some grease," the Oracle said as he spread it across the fifth-wheel plate with a piece of broken off cardboard.

We all stood near the rear of the bobtail. Grease Monkey Gary and I kept our distance as if that grease was going to fly through the air and stick to us, not that he would have noticed.

"Sure, not a problem."

"Most people might not think of this, but the front of a fully loaded semi-trailer can weigh over thirty thousand pounds. That is a lot of friction between the trailer and this plate. Keeping it well-greased gives it a noticeably smoother ride, especially for a cab-over."

"Maybe someday my meager establishment will be big enough that my shipment of new parts will take up an entire box trailer, and you can return the favor by giving me a good deal on shipping," he chuckled.

"Speaking of, do you ever wonder why Sideways Sam opened this shop so close to a much larger one?"

"No, but it works out well," he said as he turned to look at the building of his competitor next door, Edwin's Motorcycle Emporium.

"How so?" I asked.

"When I was first looking at buying this place, I thought it was crazy for him to open it right next door to the biggest dealership in the city.

"However, he knew they wouldn't work on ones that are fifteen years or older. They would send the people with the older stuff to him because he was conveniently located. He found his niche by working on crap that others wouldn't."

"This brings us to—number seventeen!"

"Seventeen!" Grease Monkey Gary yelled before I got a chance.

"There are already thousands of rock bands. Why would they need one more because you want to sing?"

"Did you change the subject?" I gave him a crazy look.

"There is already a pizza parlor on every corner. Why would they need two?"

"What?" I looked over to Grease Monkey Gary to see if he knew what was going on.

"There are already people who sell houses for a living—who needs you?"

"—but I don't want to sell real estate."

"If the lake is already full—why do they need more water?"

"Oh, I see. We're talking about demographics again."

"Yes, and sometimes in this world, there is simply no room for you—so you have to make your own. You don't have to reinvent the wheel—you only make it a little different.

"This is what's called a niche business. You look at what others are doing and try to change it to meet the needs of a select group of consumers. There may be demands in the market that nobody is meeting. By doing something a little different from others, you may fill a need that wasn't already filled."

"You mean like starting a small shop right next to a bigger one?" I again looked over at Grease Monkey Gary. This time, he shook his head in agreement.

"Sideways Sam didn't reinvent the wheel. In a market where everyone was trying to create the biggest and best shop in the area, he found his niche by creating value in an area that didn't previously exist, maintenance and sales of older bikes. And then, when he became greedy, he ripped people off until karma caught up with him."

"Presumably," I said.

"Yeah, sure. Presumably."

"Continue…"

"Alright, if you want to start a rock band, try using a distorted piano. If you want the pizza parlor, do something different from the surrounding joints. Try using a sour dough crust and tons of garlic, or make your pizzas out of recycled cardboard and sell them for two dollars each. If you want to sell real estate, buy a minivan and give ride-a-long house tours once a week. Just be different."

"I can be different."

Nothing's more different from starting a motorcycle shop in your mom's garage.

"Can I add something to this conversation?" Grease Monkey Gary asked.

"Of course, feel free…"

"Another form of a niche is a person who tries to provide a product or service superior to the competition. I thought I would compete by offering better products and service. I really think many people think like this when first starting up—it's probably because of our pride.

"Then I noticed a trend in superstores. They are becoming successful by offering crap at low prices, and people seem content with this. These places have filled a need because their customers do not want to pay for the quality product or service. They solely want a good price.

"I had to find my balance and offer excellent products along with honest service at fair prices. I can't compete with the place next door with the prices of my parts and accessories, so I have to make up for it by offering better customer service—and yes, if they have an older ride, they have nowhere else to go, so I have that going for me."

"You mentioned an important concept—balance. But we must cover another element. Hold on…" Tired of holding the greasy piece of cardboard, he walked over and threw it in the outside trash can. "Risk."

"Risk?" I asked.

"Creating a new product or finding a niche is one of the riskiest methods of starting out, because the demand you are filling might not be large enough to support your new venture financially.

"You will have limited access to market research, so you will need to compensate for this by other means of determining the level of value you will be creating. If your service provides little value for others, then you will fight a losing battle.

"If your product is a square tire or your service is dial-a-nap, then no matter how hard you attempt or how much you invest, your operation is doomed. There have been many millionaires created by finding niches, and if you find the right one, you can profit heavily from it. Yet, without an existing market to research, it is a gamble."

"Once again, showing Sideways Sam did in fact create value, value that I refinanced my house to pay for."

"Whether you are trying to compete by offering superior products, changing an existing product, or creating an invention, the risk for starting a niche business is too high. I wouldn't recommend it for starting entrepreneurs, unless they fully understand all the risks, are tough as nails, adaptable, and maybe just a little crazy."

"Crazy?" I asked.

"It wouldn't hurt." Grease Monkey Gary scratched at the back of his neck.

Baby Step #18

"It was good to meet you, Grease Monkey Gary," the Oracle said as he reached out to shake his hand.

"Be sure to look me up when you're in the area," he said as he returned the gesture.

To avoid human contact, I turned and walked around the back of the truck to get in on my side. Then, out of the corner of my eye, I caught something very unusual.

Both of them pulled a small metal case out of their back pockets, grabbed something out of them, and then exchanged these tokens—all in one fluid motion as if they were synchronized swimmers.

I continued around and climbed up into my seat, feeling my sore butt and compressed spine as I sat. The seat cushion was like a 1950s coil spring mattress that was chopped up and wrapped in leather. After a few days of riding along on this medieval torture device, I was getting trucker butt.

Satisfied with the stop, the Oracle jumped up in his seat, cranked up the motor, let it go pop, pop, pop a few times to be sure it was alive, and off we went.

It was nice to pull out on the road without a trailer. With it, we would often sit for ten or twenty minutes or more before we could find a hole in the traffic big enough to pull out into.

"Are you ready to put a lot of miles in?" He shook his coffee mug to check its level.

"Sure." I didn't want to complain even though I took notice of every coil spring in my seat jabbing at my backside.

"That's good. We have many places to be and a short time to get there."

"Can I ask you what it was that you guys exchanged back there?"

"Do you remember how I said everything is sales—even if you don't think it is?"

"Of course."

"Remember when he said that someday he would have a full shipment of parts and accessories and I'd be the first one he'd call?"

"Yes." I tried to take a sip of my brown sunshine, but without the weight of the trailer to smooth out the suspension, I found this task near impossible. That didn't matter though, it was too cold now to enjoy.

"Well, he was joking, but he was also right. He will be that big someday. What he doesn't know yet is that he will be bigger than the dealership next door and when that day comes, not only will he need parts delivered, he will also need the new vehicles hauled.

"I've been in this industry a long while now and I've known many people who have grown many businesses. I don't need a crystal ball to know who's going to make it big and who's not. Someday you're going to be driving through the area and you're going to see a massive building with the name Grease Monkey Gary's Motorcycles on it. Out back at the loading dock, you will see my truck."

"I wouldn't have thought about that."

"Which brings us to—number eighteen!"

"Eighteen!"

"What he gave me was his business card. They are essential for self-employment. Carry many with you. Give many away. Even if you don't think the person will be a client, so what? Give them one regardless. Not only does this create rapport with people, perhaps they know someone who could use your services."

"Aren't business cards so, um—1980? I remember my grandpa passing them out to everyone he met. Everybody today keeps track of each other on social media. Are they still even relevant?"

"They most definitely are. Not only do I have my name and my phone number on it like back in your grandpa's day, I also have my email address and the username of all my social media accounts so they can follow me. Instead of having a long conversation explaining to everyone how to follow me who asks, I simply hand them a card and all my information is right there."

"Did you give him one, then?" I tried to take another sip of my brown sunshine by steadying it with both hands, but still with no success.

"No, I gave him a fridge magnet with all my contact information on it, the same stuff you'd find on a card—name, number, email, and social media sites.

"It's the same concept. However, instead of having to keep track of the little piece of stiff paper, he will go into his office and stick this to the side of his filing cabinet. Then, one day when he needs me, he'll remember that's where he put it.

"Give potential clients a fridge magnet promoting your services. I have made thousands of hauls that resulted from a forty-cent fridge magnet. You want people to think of you when they need whatever it is that you offer.

"What better way to let them remember you than being eye level with them when they get the milk out of the fridge or a folder out of the filing cabinet?"

"That's actually kind of brilliant. Even if I don't yet have anything to offer, it is frustrating explaining to people how to follow me on social media. It would be nice to have all my contact information for those sites on a piece of paper, such as a card, that I could hand them. It's like a perfect blend between the old world and the new."

"Yes, remember everything is sales, even if you are not selling anything."

"Do you mind stopping at the next truck stop? I need to get a cup of hot coffee and a straw."

Chapter

Eight

"Do you enjoy surfing?" I asked the Oracle as he was looking at the surfboards hanging up on the wall.

"I don't know—never tried it."

"A surf shop is a strange place to hang out, especially since you don't surf."

"I like to look at the designs on the boards. It's practically the same as walking through an art museum. Besides, I want to keep in contact with my clients. At one time, almost everything in this shop was being pulled behind my rig."

"That's kind of cool to think of that."

After we made it to Los Angeles, the Oracle checked in with the shipyard and found out that the container that we were picking up was still on the ship. They estimated it would not be ready until three in the morning. He said that it was common when dealing with shipyards. In the meantime, we had plenty of time to kill.

"Jimmy Z and the King!" the shirtless man with a golden tan and long blonde hair shouted as he snuck up behind us.

"My dude!" the Oracle said as he did a crazy handshake with him that must've been surfer code for *I'm cool*. I've never heard him use the word dude before. "Bud, this is Bob Sandals. His beach name is the Coconut."

"I'm the assistant manager." He reached out and shook my hand in a normal way, which I took as I wasn't cool.

"Good to meet you," I replied.

"What brings you dudes into the surf shop? I wasn't expecting a load today."

"We're killing time and thought that we would come in and see what's in."

"What's in or what's *in?*"

"What's *in.*" The Oracle leaned his head back and smiled.

"We just got in these short boards over here." We followed him to the end of the row of surfboards up against the wall. "These are all handmade by a local retired surfer called Moon Dog Mike. Relish these brief visions of beauty because by closing time, they'll all be gone."

"Magnificent." The Oracle gazed at them.

"I don't get it." I confirmed that I was indeed not cool.

"What's not to get?"

"They look nice, but I don't notice a big difference between the other surfboards and them. Other than a slightly different paint scheme, which I admit is nice, they seem to be nearly identical in size and form of the other ones.

"After decades of surfing, haven't they perfected the shape of the surfboard? And if so, then would not all of them be roughly the same as the others, with possibly the exception of riding styles?"

"Yes, but they're not *in.*" The Coconut looked at me as if I wasn't cool enough to understand.

"I think what he is saying is—number nineteen!"

"Nineteen!"

"Nineteen!" The Coconut went along, though he didn't know why.

"The eighty-twenty rule is basically that, what's *in,* is what's *in.*"

"Yeah, dude."

"When you create an item or service that the majority wants, you are *in.* Twenty percent of the real estate agents sell eighty percent of the homes. If you make a product whose value is in the top twenty percentile, you'll get eighty percent of the marketplace.

"Today, the majority of the surfboards the Coconut sells will come out of this selection of designs made by Moon Dog Mike. That means that if you are the maker of these others, then you'll need to compete with all the other *not in* manufactures for the remaining measly sales."

"Hold on—I could see how this rule applies to things that are trendy, such as a shop or a clothing store. I also understand how it may be relevant to trades that require skills, as in real estate agents—since the top dogs would most likely possess the most skill, therefore creating the greatest value to their clients, but I don't see where else this relates?"

"That is true. The rule does not apply to every service or product. It is a common enough phenomenon, however, that you should know it.

"Think of Grease Monkey Gary's motorcycle shop—if a biker drives over to that section of town, he only has a twenty percent chance they may go into his shop versus the big one next-door. He has to adjust all of his expenses in order to stay afloat and break a profit."

"How can he adjust to such a meager share of the market?"

"By following the eighty-twenty rule within his operation. Almost all the services which he performs will most likely be from a small fraction of the actual services he provides.

"Despite the wide range of maintenance and repairs he offers, most of the work he carries out are oil changes, tune-ups, cleaning carbs, and changing tires. So much so that he will be overjoyed when someone comes in with a blown motor.

"The same goes for the products he sells—even though many parts and accessories littered his walls, eighty percent of his sales might come from just a few of them. He may sell spark plugs and quarts of oil to almost everyone who walks through the door, and occasionally sell handlebars and fenders to those who don't know how to ride.

"The reason why knowing this rule is important is that if your entire market share is within the lower percentile, then you need to learn how to survive inside of that limitation or to be more competitive to take a bigger slice of the pie.

"As for your products, it's critical you know which *in* items are bringing in the most revenue and advertise and push sales towards them to get the greatest investment for your money."

"Yeah, dude. You don't even have to be cool to be *in*." The Coconut ran his hand down the smooth edge of one of the Moon Dog Mike boards.

"You simply have to be competitive," the Oracle added.

Baby Step #20

"Wow, this is amazing! There's nothing but a faint line between the horizon of the ocean and the sky. It's almost as if they blend together. To see all those ships so far out and yet still be visible—they must be enormous!" I said as we sat on the end of this old pier. How it moaned as the waves lunged under it, I was unsure if it was still safe. Surely it passed a peer safety certification, if there is such a thing. *Eek.*

"Yep, pretty amazing."

"You don't seem very excited."

"I can't say that I am, really. While watching the sun go down is always entertaining, it's that after you see the sunset over the ocean in Mazatlán, well, everyplace else is totally—blah."

"Seriously? It's better than this?"

"It can't be explained to anybody who hasn't experienced it themselves. But do you know what it can explain?"

"What's that?"

"Number twenty!"

"Twenty!"

"You are the most vital part of your business. It would be nothing without you. You create it and, without knowing yourself, you may be the one to destroy it. You better have a master's degree in yourself before you start any course or pick up even a single book."

"That sounds like common sense. You brought me all the way out here to teach me that?"

"It is common sense. In fact, most of what I'm teaching you might challenge your basic logic. Every decision you make, common sense or not, comes from within you.

"It's similar to being a captain of one of those ships way out on the ocean. It would appear that with nothing more than a steering wheel and a throttle, that all of their decisions shouldn't be complex. Spin the wheel and adjust the throttle in the correct combination to get from point A to point B safely. But is it really that simple?"

"With the training they go through and the experience required—I would say most definitely not."

"Exactly, and if you undertake this endeavor without self-knowledge, you may well be a naïve fool at the helm of a ship—I hope somebody will be there to save you when the ship goes down."

"I get it. So many young entrepreneurs study business through books, and they should, but not at the expense of also studying within themselves."

"Wow—I should've totally said it that way." He glanced over at me with a look on his face that I assumed was pride.

Baby Step #21

When I stood there in the truck stop parking lot back home, there were two versions of me. The first version was the failure that lived at home and wouldn't talk to his friends because he was embarrassed. I hid in my bedroom day after day, trying to hide from the world, but it was actually myself and who I had become that I was hiding from.

The second version was the kid who picked up his gym bag and took that first step. I am here now riding in this truck because that version of me showed up. No longer do I need to hide from my life. I am strong enough. I am fast enough. I am smart enough. I am the person who steps forward. I am the person who succeeds!

Glum Goblin, it should be you who packs up his bags.

"So, this is head gasket hill?" I asked, taking my attention off from the trees slowly drifting by.

We were hauling a forty-foot container box on a skeletal trailer heading for Nebraska and were traveling at about half the speed of ooze being squeezed out of a crack. This time the motor sounded like some fool put a handful of marbles in an empty can and put it in a paint shaker down at the local hardware store.

"It is," he muffled as he chewed the last few bites of his peanut butter and jelly sandwich. Making that while he was driving showed how truly talented of a driver he was, regardless of the speed.

"This sure gives a young man like myself loads of time to chew on his thoughts."

"There are a few things I'm chewing on myself."

"Such as?"

"Think about this, technically we are driving through the Wild Wild West. A little over a couple of hundred years ago, there was nothing on this hill but perhaps a few lost coyotes. Of course, there are a couple of ghost towns scattered about to remind us that some humans did indeed live out here, but there is a bunch of land between them that never had a human footprint on it."

"The Wild West sure has changed." I looked back out at the scenery.

"This brings up the point that we are merely climbing this hill because I am following the people who traveled it before me. Before this road was ever here, an explorer walked up it, maybe to find an alternative route, maybe to find a new adventure, or maybe solely to see what's on the other side. Maybe he was on horseback, maybe not.

"One thing is for sure is that at some moment after that, someone decided they wanted to take a wagon up it. Slowly, painstakingly, before big machinery, they chiseled out a dirt path. That path turned into a dirt road which widened, then they added asphalt, then it widened even more, and now it is the road that we drive on. If it was not for whom we follow, this road would not exist and what used to take days or weeks now only takes a few hours."

"I guess I should be grateful for how fast we are traveling."

"Which brings us to—number twenty-one!"

"Twenty-one!"

"If you were to hike up a mountain, which would be the easiest way—making your own trail or following the beaten-down path?"

"Taking the path—of course."

"Realize the old have already blazed the trail for the young to follow. This allows the youth to travel quickly and surpass those who created it. If someone achieved a skill at age forty-five, then the successor may succeed by age thirty." He downshifted another gear.

Any more downshifting and I fear we could possibly come to a complete stop.

"I see what you're saying. If anything has been done before, then I should be able to do it faster than the person who did it the first time—but how? I know college helped me go in that direction, though there's undeniably something missing."

"Formal education is important to learn the fundamentals, although only five percent of a good business mind comes from schooling—the rest must be observed." He casually took a sip of coffee as a carload of young adults passed us, honking their horn and flipping us off.

"That's a bold statement. You make it sound as if it wasn't worth the tuition."

"Sometimes it is, sometimes it isn't. Whether or not you're formally educated, it is essential that you find someone in the position you would like to be in. You can follow their trail while using your best judgment to avoid the same mistakes. Use these people as trail leaders to show you the way.

"Mentors are easy to find and typically give useful advice and guidance. One of the greatest things I found in most MLMs and real estate offices is that they usually assign a mentor to you until you figure things out for yourself. Large organizations know you are more likely to succeed with a guide."

"It seems like having one is a tremendous advantage to someone like me just beginning the journey—won't there come a point where my mentor can only take me so far?"

I must admit that the higher we climb, the better the view is of the valley off to our left-hand side.

"That is a genuine possibility. To exceed your current advisor, you should seek a different one that can take you farther. You may notice that before you achieve your goal, that mentors are rarer near the top and less willing to give advice.

"Afterwards, you must take it upon yourself to forge your own trail. By doing this, you'll become a leader and others will have a tendency to follow your path."

"Me, a leader? That seems to be a really long road to travel down from where I'm at now."

"One thing I learned about driving truck, no matter how lengthy the route, you always get there eventually. You simply need a strong cup of coffee and persistence."

Chapter

Nine

After we dropped the forty-foot container and skeletal trailer in Omaha, our next stop was to pick up a flatbed with hay about a hundred miles south of there. It didn't take long after leaving before we found ourselves in farmland.

When we arrived at the following location, the Johnson farm, we found out that rain had delayed the farmer from being able to access the field to cut the hay. That left him scrambling to get it loaded before we showed up. We didn't mind, though. His wife, from a generation that wore aprons, greeted us at the door with iced tea.

This skyrocketed the credibility of the Oracle's teachings. Anyone who's never lounged on a front porch sipping iced tea and gazing out over a farmer's field has no right to give advice to anybody else.

The Oracle sat his empty glass down on the porch, looked up over at me and said, "One major struggle in business is managing your bitches and hoes."

"Whafpt!" I filled my lungs to the brim with farm fresh tea as I swallowed down the wrong tube. I rushed over to the edge of the porch, where mixed fluids erupted out of my mouth and nose.

"What?"

"Wha…" I tried to get out as I took my free hand and wiped off my face with the bottom of my shirt, careful not to spill the remaining of my cup.

"What?"

"That's kind of sexist, isn't it?" My voice crackled as air was attempting to push out the remaining liquid in my lungs. I sat back in my wicker chair and took deep breaths.

"Ha! That's not what I meant. I was talking about that dog hopping around in the front yard and the plow that gets pulled behind the tractor to dig up dirt."

He pointed to the golden retriever puppy playing on the small patch of grass. Farmers are good at growing everything, but a good front lawn.

"Are you absolutely positive about that? It seems to me that there would be a better way to say the same thing?"

"Of course—no man with as many daughters as I have could ever be sexist."

"I didn't know you had kids?" I walked over to the handrail again, to hack up more lung tea.

"My friends are my family and their kids are my kids. There are not any of those children that I don't watch over as if they are my own."

"Then how about instead of using the words bitches and hoe's, grammatically accurate as they are—why don't we just say dogs and tractors?" Once again taking my seat and quickly taking another sip.

"Seems reasonable—then on to number twenty-two!"

"Twenty-two!" I shouted, finally in agreement with the lesson's terminology.

"A tractor is nothing high or glamorous. It simply chugs away at plowing up the ground. You never see farmers gloating at their progress or trying to impress anybody with their hard labor. Farmers notice what needs to be done, fires up the tractor, and quietly toil away at their end goal of raising a crop."

"Yes—the term tractor is more appropriate."

"A classic example of a *tractor* is my good buddy, Truck Stop Tom. At thirty-seven years old, he owns the largest truck stop in Utah.

"He drives an old pickup truck and runs around the station on a golf cart with a toilet plunger mounted on the back. He wears a pair of undersized orange flip-flop sandals and never has on a shirt."

"That's quite the visual." This caused my face to squinch.

"I tinkered on his golf cart because he wanted it to be faster. You can get them to go over thirty miles per hour by merely tuning the engine right. With his place consisting of an abundance of loose gravel and this additional horsepower, he could drift the rear end sideways on the turns—same as a flat-track racer."

"I can see that toilet plunger needing a good holder to keep it from flying off."

"Eventually, a driver complained to the manager about the maintenance man speeding. He wanted him to be fired immedi-

ately. The manager had a hard time not laughing—she couldn't figure out how to explain that she didn't hold the authority to fire the owner."

"That would be something."

"Truck Stop Tom is the first person you see in the back lot filling in potholes with a shovel or walking into the restrooms with a plunger. He is not interested in showing how hard he works. He does whatever it takes to be successful and keep the place running. Simply put, he just gets the job done. He currently holds millions of dollars in real estate investments and one old pickup truck."

"He sounds like a buddy I'd hang around with."

"The dog, unlike the tractor, yaps a lot and chases her tail while getting nothing accomplished."

"Hold on, is it necessary the four-legged friend has to be a she?"

"In this case of that yellow big eared puppy out on the lawn, that is the accurate pronoun."

"Fair. Continue."

"She, regarding to this particular dog," he indicated to floppy, a nickname I made for her, "stands out more than the tractor and to onlookers, it may appear as if she is getting more accomplished because she is furiously chasing that tail. Other than minor accomplishments, they will achieve no noticeable gain.

"Both men and women who must dress in fashionable attire and drive luxurious cars to impress others are purely dogs that yap a lot. Dogs tend to not stay in the industry for very long."

"Despite a shaky beginning, you made a good point."

"As they put it on the farm, let's cut through all the fluff. Instead of wearing formal business attire, dress as an equal—not above your customers, team members, and colleagues. You wouldn't try to dress above your classmates, would you?"

"Not really, maybe a nicer shirt."

"There is a psychology behind the clothing you wear. The message you give by dressing up, instead of with, is that you are superior to them. The only intent of a suit is to create a prestige suggestion, which gives the wearer more perceived power. That is the sole purpose of the suit. There is no other reasonable utility." He finished his glass and sat it on the porch.

Reasonable utility?

"To keep us from being naked?"

"There are better ways to prevent that. The power of dressing above others creates an advantage in financial transactions such as sales—individuals are more likely to accept suggestions from perceived superiors. If the transaction is fair, why would you need to manipulate others with the clothes you wear?"

"That's something to consider." I took the last swallow of my tea and sat my glass next to his.

"There are many areas of business where the fundamentals of manipulation seep. You should behave as one mature person to another and you should appear equal. This doesn't mean that you can't still look nice and dignified, though."

"What if, while attempting to create rapport with your team by wearing similar clothing as them, you are called to negotiations with a suit wearer?"

"One way of dealing with this situation is to keep a suit at your office or a sports coat within arm's reach. A sports coat fancies up while going with most anything else you are wearing."

"People still wear those?"

"I can't really say. I am convinced that a suit will not make you appear better if you are already secure in yourself. If you are insecure, then swanky clothes will not cover it up.

"If you enter a room standing tall and reflecting absolute confidence, walking up to the other party and giving a firm handshake while making eye contact, most of them will shake in their shoes."

"Nothing beats good old-fashioned self-esteem."

I wish my glass wasn't empty.

"Regarding the expensive cars and striving to impress others with your wealth, I reckon this is the exact opposite of what you should do with your money.

"There was a couple I met at a tavern who were bragging about how they recently opened a trucking company in town. The guy was a prime example of a dog. He undoubtfully spent hundreds of dollars buying folks drinks to show that he had financial means. You could see his insecurities a mile away—even his wife gawked at him as if he was a moron.

"When the night had finished, none of these people knew that as an owner operator, I was the most lucrative businessperson in the trucking industry in that bar. I didn't see how it was any of their concern. None of them would ever need my services.

"Nobody cared who they were or what they owned. They maintained operations for about a year and a half and I am still doing what I do."

"There were a few braggers in school. I always assumed that they grew out of it."

"They only get worse."

"Excuse me…" The wicked side of drinking too much tea was creeping up on me.

Baby Step #23

When we dropped off the flatbed full of hay, we picked up an empty reefer trailer and dead headed over to downtown Milwaukee. Despite the warehouse not opening for another three hours, we arrived early and backed up to the receiving dock.

On the street corner across from us were two, to put it politely, ladies of the night, one of which walked our way no sooner than he popped the air brakes on the Beast. I locked my door.

She then persisted in climbing up the steps on his side and put her arms against the bottom of the window to hold herself up the best she could. "Hey sweet thing—what are you needing tonight?" she asked with a phony Jersey accent.

"What do you think a guy like me is looking for at four in the morning?" he said to the lady.

"Oh… You're so dirty. I'll wait for you down the alley," she said and then glanced over at me, "and bring your friend.

I could use the company." She awkwardly leaned in and kissed him on the cheek, climbed down and headed towards the alley.

"You coming?" he asked as he rolled up his window to lock up.

"No way!"

I'll say this about him, he lives a diverse life. One minute he's sitting on the front porch drinking iced tea, the next he is walking into a lightless alleyway with a prostitute.

"Suit yourself. Definitely keep your door locked. It's a rough neighborhood." He popped open his door.

"Hold on!" I quickly hopped out of the Beast and sprinted around the front to make certain I caught him before he faded into the evil shadows of the city—leaving me to go in there alone.

"You worry too much. There's nothing quite so tranquil than the inner city at night. It's almost like we own the entire place—as if the day dwellers surrendered it to us," he said.

"I have to ask you—is this one of the lessons?"

"Why do you ask that?"

"Well, back at the farm, you used the metaphor of a bitch and a hoe, which was accurate considering that it was indeed a female dog and a plow being pulled behind a tractor—despite there being a more appropriate manner to describe those same things. Now, here we are meandering in the midst of night and the first thing we see are two call girls. Please don't tell me this is about bitches and hos."

"Ha! You are spot on about that last metaphor. I should've said the dog and the farmer initially. But you're mistaken about my friend who labors the night-shift of love. I would never use those words to describe a woman—regardless of their profession."

"Good," I said as we entered the backstreet.

There, waiting for us, leaning against the wall and nervously trying to light a cigarette, was his lady friend.

"I don't think I introduced you two—this is Go-Getter Gabby, Go-Getter Gabby… This is Bud."

"Pleasure to meet you."

I'm still scared about being in a dimly lit alley. Nothing good ever happens in the dark.

"Pleasure to meet you, too. Are you ready for this?" Her flirting caused her accent to crack.

"Maybe?" Did my face turn pale or blush? I couldn't tell for sure. I was solely thankful it was hidden by the night.

"Well then, let's go." She turned and started walking further down the alley, her high heels echoed against the bricks of the buildings and disappeared into the empty air.

He quickly walked behind her, leaving me standing there alone. Unsure of what was happening, I remained frozen. I saw both their silhouettes turn the corner at the backstreet's other end.

I gasped for a second and then ran to catch up. My dignity couldn't keep up with how fast I was running. As I turned the corner, I saw both of them enter the all-night diner.

Suddenly, I felt much better about the moment.

*

"Well, well, well… If it isn't Jimmy Z and Go-Getter Gabby. I don't believe I've had the honor of meeting this young man," the waitress said as she winked over at me.

Chapter Nine

Without even asking if we wanted coffee, she slid out three cups and filled them.

The diner was just as expected for an all-night city joint. The worn seat cushions had rips in them, not to mention the entire place smelled of cigarette smoke that still lingered from 1978.

I slid in on one side of the booth, followed by the Oracle, and Go-Getter Gabby sat on the other side. The steam of my brown sunshine marked my territory.

"I'm Bud."

I had to lean down to suck a little brown sunshine out of my cup after I poured five packets of sugar and three creamers into it, afraid that it would overflow if I picked it up. It was obviously strong by how it flowed coming out of the pot.

"Bud, what are we going to have tonight?" She pulled the ticket book out of the front pocket of her server apron.

"Just fries, please."

"Just fries it is. What about you, Jimmy Z? Is it breakfast or dinner?"

"It's hard to tell. Let's play it safe. Bring me an omelet with some broccoli in it."

"Yes sir, one Jimmy Z special," she said as she wrote it down, "and only coffee for you again?"

"Yes, sweetie," Go-Getter Gabby said as the waitress turned and rushed off.

"Go-Getter Gabby, why didn't you invite your friend to come with us?" I asked.

The Oracle focused on drinking his coffee.

"You mean Big Shot Brenda? She is not my friend! That girl wears too much makeup." She doubled the thickness of her fake Jersey accent.

"Sorry, I thought you were friends because you were hanging out together."

"That girl makes us all look bad. She needs to find her own corner."

"How is that so?" I innocently took a sip off of my brown sunshine.

"She is an amateur—I am an entrepreneur!"

"What classifies someone as an amateur versus someone as an entrepreneur?"

"Care if I answer this, Go-Getter Gabby?" the Oracle asked.

"Be my guest."

"Okay, then—number twenty-three!"

"Twenty-three!"

"An amateur will be in the ladies' room fixing her makeup, while an entrepreneur will be out working her stuff."

"To clarify, all of us, regardless of gender, ethnicity, form, or height are either an entrepreneur or an amateur, correct?" I asked.

"Of course, professionalism knows no boundaries." He glanced over at me as though it were a ridiculous question.

"Very well then."

"The activities of the amateur are tedious tasks that are required for the business to operate, but they do not directly make it any money.

"Setting the desk, cleaning the office, delivering checks for the bills, bookkeeping, upkeep of machinery or buildings, putting things in place where they belong, replying to letters and e-mails, constructing shelves, making non-sale or non-prospecting related calls, shipping, running errands, making coffee, organizing, striving to improve things that don't need improving, and so forth—it's all *amateur work*. Necessary? Yes, but by doing these things, nobody miraculously appears and gives you a fistful of cash."

"Just like Big Shot Brenda," Go-Getter Gabby interrupted, "always wasting all that time shopping for shoes."

"The entrepreneur, however, will go out and do things that directly result in the opportunity to make a profit. They may prospect, knock on doors, market and advertise, call potential clients and ask them if they could use a service, get face-to-face with customers—no matter what it takes. These are the go getters that drive the business to profitability."

"That's me, always prospecting, always searching for my next John."

"The amateur work may be necessary, but it'll put you out of the game in a hurry. New small business owners and real estate agents can easily observe this. They look busy as hell doing the amateur work, but they make no money.

"New real estate agents run round and round the office frantically, tidying their desks, connecting with their mortgage brokers, chasing after staples, changing their day planners for when they might need more staples, and then taking a break to unwind. Only one in sixty real estate associates makes it the first year."

"One out of sixty?" I looked over at him.

"And if you think that's tough, try being a call girl. That's why I never take time to clean my office," she said.

"You rent an office?" I glanced over at her.

"Sure do. Where else would I go to keep my billing straight and store my contacts? I have a mailing list to build, a website to maintain, and all my social media sites are growing every day.

"Me and the girls even put out a seasonal postcard where we all prettied up—except we don't invite Big Shot Brenda to be in it. We don't want her face making it look all trashy."

"I never thought of that."

"At my place," her accent completely disappeared, "a messy desk is a certain sign of productivity. You can see the path of my destruction, almost like a tornado followed me.

"Then, at the end of the day or the next morning, I take a few minutes to put things back where they go. This is to prevent not being able to find things and slowing my progress.

"I carefully watch that my focus is on *entrepreneur work*. I keep telling myself that I didn't quit that job as a computer programmer just so I'd have time to walk back-and-forth drinking coffee."

"You were a computer programmer?" I sat my cup down on the table.

"I was, but if you think my boss now has a temper, try working with Kyle from accounting." Her accent returned.

"That's interesting."

"I'm just here to add value to this world the best way I know how and ask for a fair compensation in return. What part of running about and shopping for shoes adds direct value to my John's?"

"Wow, I never knew that your profession was so complex."

"That is why I hired Trash Talker Tina. "

"You have an employee?"

"Yes, to keep me from being constantly sidetracked by my amateur work, other than simply avoiding it, I hired an assistant to handle these insignificant jobs for me. This gives me more time on the street, doing what I do to earn a living."

"What if I can't afford an employee?"

"If you are in the beginning stages," he said, "then you are right. It's hard to pay for an assistant when you only make a couple of sales a year, if you're lucky. But if you can afford a helper, then you might want to consider it.

"If you bring in about twenty-seven dollars an hour because of prospecting, then you can hire an assistant for eighteen an hour to do the amateur work for you. This gives you a chance to fully use your talent while ensuring that you profit nine bucks an hour off their labor.

"Consider this, though—can you prospect and do the entrepreneur work the entire day or by hiring an assistant, would it merely allow you to take naps? Do you need your amateur work to balance your entrepreneur work?"

"That would be tough, doing nothing but entrepreneur work all day long." I picked up my cup by the sides in order to warm my hands a little. The diner was a few degrees cooler than comfortable.

"I'm not saying it should be your aim to rid yourself of all the amateur work," he continued. "That may not serve you well. However, frankly, I want it to come to your attention that if amateur work is all you do—you are doomed. Most people are guilty of this.

"Find a balance that still propels your enterprise forward. Prioritize your entrepreneur work and don't let the amateur work take from that schedule."

"When I was first starting…" She lost her accent again. I tried not to laugh. "I knew I had to spend most of my efforts prospecting and doing entrepreneur work. It's very competitive out there. Every day it seems like there are more college girls that can't make tuition.

"In order to gain the edge and make certain I wasn't wasting unnecessary time on amateur work, I created a list with two columns—in one column I documented my average daily activities that were entrepreneur work and in the second column, I noted my amateur work.

"By comparing the columns, I asked myself if I was an amateur or an entrepreneur? My answer shocked me. It completely altered the way I went about my job."

"I bet that exercise was a real eye-opener," he commented.

"Of course, it was. I learned it from you."

"All right, here we have a Jimmy Z special and an order of just fries." The waitress winked at me as she slid our breakfast, or dinner, or whatever in front of us.

Chapter

Ten

Baby Step #24

"Come on, get in," the Oracle yelled over at me while hanging his arm out of a brand-new metallic blue pickup truck.

It had a diesel motor but sounded nothing like the Beast. It was more similar to a sewing machine effortlessly trying to sew together two pieces of silk.

After leaving Milwaukee, we found ourselves in Michigan picking up an automobile transport trailer full of top-of-the-line vehicles leaving the factory. That brought us to Colorado to this dealership.

I was keeping my distance while he worked. The transporter had two levels. After the lower part was unloaded, he flipped a few levers and the upper level lowered.

I fit into a very special demographic, one that would lead me to be the probable subject of a newspaper line that said, 'kid crushed by hydraulic cylinders in a freak transport trailer accident.'

A group of sales attendants came out to pull the deliveries around back by the shop where they were to be gone through by the mechanics and then given a final detail before going on the lot. He decided to park this one personally as an excuse to drive it.

"This is nice," I said as I hopped in.

The first thing I noticed was that the odometer only had nine miles on it. There was plastic that still covered the seats, and the King fit comfortably within the massive cup holders. Also, other than a few dirty shoe prints on the carpet, it was clean enough to do surgery in—if the need arose.

"What do you think? Can you see me driving something like this?" he asked as if seeking permission to buy it.

He rolled up his window and started driving it slightly above walking speed, as if he was afraid to scratch it.

"Possibly."

I'm not sure what his financial situation is, but I certainly don't want to be the person making the payments on it.

"If you didn't know me and saw me drive this down the road—what could you assume about me?"

"I don't know."

"Paint a picture of what you think my life would be like."

"I would say that you are successful—the type of person who would have one of them big houses, you know, those big ones with stucco and a two-car garage, plush green grass, perhaps a few trees out front for decoration, and outback a small deck with a hot tub."

"Good visual. Do you know what I think when I see somebody driving this type of truck down the road?"

"No."

"I see someone who is a weak competitor, and, even worse, a fragile entrepreneur. Someone who is in a constant state of quiet desperation. Someone who is a single missed payment away from returning to the job at the factory from which they came from."

Weak competitor? Fragile entrepreneur?

"I'm glad the windows are up—somebody might've heard you say that."

"The people who would be offended by that are the people who need to hear it the most."

"Really?" I instinctively looked over to make sure my window actually was up.

"The biggest mistake I see people who are starting out is to under-finance their business and over-finance their personal lives, fancy cars, big houses, a hot tub.

"It's hard to keep things going when you don't have enough money—it's a double slap in the face when it's your mortgage, car payments, and credit cards that are taking all of your capital."

"But isn't keeping up an appearance part of the deal?"

"Sideways Sam used to race bullet bikes long before he ever owned a motorcycle shop. Back then they called him Sideways Sam because he would slide sideways in all the turns. The nickname was coincidently convenient later on when he was a shady businessman.

"I remember going to a few events with him back then. Before the race, the staging area was littered with everybody polishing the dust off their freshly purchased state-of-the-art motorcycle. And then there was his bike…

"When he began racing it, it didn't look too bad. It was definitely a little older than the other ones, but still in great shape for its age. After a few races and crashes, much of the plastic fairing was riveted together or patched with duct tape. A few more races later—not a stitch of plastic could be found."

"Was that safe?"

"For a motorcycle to run, all that it really needs is two wheels connected by a frame with a motor in it. Typically, all the unnecessary stuff flies off the first time you cartwheel it."

"Really?" *Cartwheel?*

"When they all lined up for the beginning of the race, nobody wanted to be next to him. They knew he wasn't afraid to scratch his bike if that meant he could win the race—and he wasn't afraid to scratch their bikes if they got in his path.

"By buying the latest of motorcycles, ones that they were afraid to damage because they still had six years of payments left to make on, made them weak competitors. Having a bike of no value made him dangerously fast.

"You see, sometimes giving the impression to others that you have more money than they do compromises your true strength and ultimately jeopardizes your chances of winning the race."

"Again, I'm glad the windows are rolled up. I'm sure there's many people who don't want to hear that either."

"In my industry, I don't give much notice to those rookie drivers who go out and buy a pristine truck with a custom paint job and matching trailer. Times get tough, even in trucking. When businesses slow down, we slow down. When the over-leveraged rookies slow down—they tend to disappear.

"Truckers have a tendency to drop like flies during an economic recession. Three months of not earning enough money to make the payment could leave the owner sitting on the curb.

"The people I worry about as competition are the ones that drive the old rigs with maybe a missing fender, maybe bald tires, maybe a knocking motor."

"Same as your truck?"

"Exactly—the thing that made me a weak entrepreneur in the beginning was my personal debt. More than once, I had to abandon my driving to earn a normal paycheck.

"The thing that makes me a strong entrepreneur now is not having any of those financial obligations and figuring out ways to run my business without it when times are lean. With very little outgo, I only need a little income to keep the wheels rolling.

"Debt does not compromise my driving. The only reason I would have to give it up is if the income wasn't higher than the base operating costs. When times are that bad, it only means I can sleep in longer."

"Wow, a business without collectors knocking on the door. How would that be…" I caught myself still eyeing the rows of brand-new, shiny, beautiful, rolling shit boxes—waiting patiently there to lure in my competitors and weaken them.

"Which brings us to—number twenty-four!"

"Twenty-four!"

"Work hard to get out of personal debt because it will directly jeopardize your chances of success. Making a buck is thrilling—until it's used to pay your obligations, of which you might only secure one extra month of time."

"You're probably right—perhaps we should roll down our windows so more people can hear it."

Baby Step #25

"Well, if it's not my old friend Jimmy Z and his trusty sidekick, the King!" the man with a polyester suit and a recent, however cheap, haircut with matching thick mustache said as he shook the Oracle's hand.

I took a few steps back.

After we unloaded, we had to go inside to drop off some paperwork for the billing. We made the mistake of looking at a red convertible on the showroom floor for too long and attracting a sales associate. Never trust a man with a thick mustache. Never.

"Fast Freddie! How are sales going?"

"They'd be a little better if you drove this home tonight." He tapped the hood of the convertible.

"Ha! Not likely."

"Why do they call you Fast Freddie?" I asked.

"Because I drive real fast." He smiled.

"It's because he talks real fast," the Oracle corrected him.

"Tell me, Jimmy Z, what would it take to put you into that car tonight?"

"I'm sure you're wasting your time with him!" I unintentionally laughed out loud.

"Why is that?" he asked.

"A second ago, I got a ten-minute lecture on how financing a luxury you don't need in life makes you a weaker competitor and more vulnerable to fail."

"I know Jimmy Z well enough to know that if he really wanted this fine piece of American engineering, he wouldn't need to finance it."

"He makes a good point. If you can come up with cash for it, would it still make you a vulnerable entrepreneur?" I asked.

"Good question, one deserving of a Baby Step number. So—number twenty-five!"

"Twenty-five!"

"Avoid too many comforts and indulgences until you have paid off everything that controls you. By having them, not only are you exchanging valuable hours of your life to pay for it, but also to cover the interest on it. Ask yourself—what is the true cost of the borrowed money? How many hours of life do I have to exchange for that money?

"Therefore, we have to ask, is spending a dollar only costing you a dollar? Consider it this way—instead of spending your dollar on a bag of cheesy chips, you put it towards your mortgage. Over the duration of your mortgage, you save $1.22 in interest.

"Now, by spending that dollar in your pocket elsewhere instead of paying down your mortgage, it is costing you $1.22 in interest—bringing the total cost of your cheesy chips to a whopping $2.22. Are cheesy chips worth that much? What about this new convertible? Even if I paid cash for it, how much is it costing me by not paying down debt elsewhere?"

"I would say that it costs you about two and a half times what the sticker price is?" I estimated.

"And the true cost of the other expenses of it would also be two and a half times their original amount, sales tax, insurance, everything."

"Hold on," fast Freddie interrupted, "you don't have a mortgage. In fact, I know you don't so much as have a credit card. It's not in your nature."

"Uh…"

"Yeah, that is a good point. What if an individual arrived with money in hand and no other financial responsibility—would it be acceptable for them to purchase it then?" I asked.

"Remember, they are still trading the security of their business for it. The more they put out towards that vehicle, the less they'll have in their bank to cover unforeseen expenses."

"Okay, what if they are not a struggling business mogul, came in with a pocket full of cash and no other obligations?" Fast Freddie asked as if he was challenging someone to a duel.

"If this is all they expect out of life, had no dreams or passions, were satisfied with empty pleasures, then sure, why not?"

I guess nice time is over…

A young couple from across the showroom floor looked over at us. I casually moved a few more steps back. "You shouldn't say that so loudly. I think those people over there heard."

"Again, those who are most offended by that statement are those who probably need to hear it the most."

Baby Step #26:

"Excuse me, sir," the woman from the young couple across the showroom floor said as they approached us, "our ride keeps breaking down and my husband thinks that since we are still making payments on it, we might as well trade it in on something that runs. I think we should pay down our current loans first and I caught your conversation from over there."

They were in their early thirties, but I called them a young couple because they looked recently married.

"Yeah, having a payment is just a part of being a responsible driver. When it starts going to the shop, you might as well go buy something fresh off the assembly line and save yourself all the hassle," he touted in the same manner as an eighth-grade science teacher who's trying to explain gravity… It makes little sense, but it is the way it is—so deal with it.

"Here's my card." Fast Freddie pulled a card out of his pocket so fast it appeared as if he was training to be a magician.

"If we wanted to get out of debt quickly, how would you suggest we go about it?" she asked.

"It is as easy as outgo verses income. Don't spend more than you earn. If you are already in too deep by not following that simple rule, then try following this even simpler one—spend even less or earn more," the Oracle said as the man laughed a little because he thought it was unrealistic.

"Could you be more specific?" the woman asked.

"Sure—number twenty-six!" he shouted, catching everyone off guard except me—who was used to it by now.

"Twenty-six!" I joined in.

"What? What's twenty-six?" the man asked.

"Try this idea—come up with an extra hundred bucks per month, either by reducing your spending or by getting a second job. Take that and put it towards the credit card with the lowest balance. How much is the monthly payment of the one that you have?"

"I have a credit card with a payment of forty-four dollars."

"Let's say that not only do you pay the forty-four dollars, you also include the added hundred. The extra amount will go directly towards the balance. Keep doing this until it's completely paid off. What is the payment for your next lowest one?"

"I have one with a monthly payment of one hundred and thirty-two."

"Now take the entire one hundred and forty-four that went towards the first card and apply it to this. You pay the one thirty-two as usual. On top of that amount, add the other for a payment total of two hundred and seventy-six.

"Once you settle that off, you add the two hundred and seventy-six on top of your regular car payment. Then after you're done with that, take the excess and apply it toward your other vehicle, that is, if you each have one. When you have those paid off, take the total amount that you are now saving and put it all towards the house payment."

"You mean pay off the house, too?" She looked as if somebody was trying to sell her magic beans.

"Yes, if you had a thirty-year mortgage and made double payments, you might possibly pay it off in around nine or ten years. By using this plan, you can go from up to your eyeballs in creditors to being completely debt-free, including your mortgage, in a little over ten years. Some people can do it in less. It all starts with changing your *outgo versus income* by a hundred bucks."

The man counted on his fingers and it looked as if it all added up. "Wow—when we make it home, we'll sit down with a calculator and create a financial plan using this strategy to figure out how long it would take for us to do that."

"Thank you so much!" She shook the Oracle's hand as they turned and walked away.

I nonchalantly walked to the other side of the convertible, no use risking the hit-by-pitch handshake by standing too close.

"Since you cost me a sale—do you have a hundred I can borrow? I'm going to give that a try." Fast Freddie held out his hand.

"You realize you can't pay off your debt by borrowing more money—right?"

Baby Step #27

"I really don't like this place—it reminds me of high school," I said as we pulled through the security gates.

A maze of fourteen-foot-high chain-link fences with coiled barbed wire surrounded us. Buildings made entirely of concrete with tinted black windows were scattered about like a handful of oversized dice.

"Yeah, I remember the first correctional facility I delivered to. It was very unnerving, but somebody has to deliver that shipment of meat-like byproduct so the prisoners can eat."

"I bet that this prison relates to whatever today's Baby Steps lesson is about." I couldn't help but stare at the buildings, as unnerving as they were.

"Why do you say that?"

"We were recently talking about debt at the dealership and now we're delivering a load to prison. It seems relatable."

"It does?"

"Well, anyhow, I must say that it was a nice thing you did for that couple back there."

"What did I do?"

"You know, teaching them the easy way to get the bankers off their backs. I bet they'll enjoy their freedom."

"But did I change anything?" He looked over at me with a serious face.

"What do you mean?"

"They were not ready for the whole truth. In fact, they were not ready for what truth I did tell them."

"What is the whole truth?"

Even with the prison yards fifteen mile-per-hour speed limit, it seemed as if it was only minutes before we were backing up to their docks. There were two men with shaved heads, one with a face tattoo, and a pallet jack standing there waiting to unload it. In the kitchen, they don't have to wear hairnets if they have no hair.

"There is a euphoric feeling associated with spending money. Buying things makes people happy. When times are bad, we would do almost anything to feel any sense of euphoria, especially getting new crap. This is actually an addiction.

"Even though I talked them out of buying something today, the next time he has a bad day, he'll come home and mention that they should just go look at cars—you know, for fun.

"She might possibly be having a bad day too and cave-in. A few hours later, they will drive home a new set of wheels. All that I accomplished today was costing Fast Freddie a sale."

He hopped out of the Beast to go open the trailer doors for the kitchen workers. Despite my better judgment, I followed.

"You're saying that there is no possibility that they are ever going to taste freedom?" I asked while we waited for the kitchen workers to pop the load lock.

"Let's say that they do. Let's say that they follow my advice and struggle and scrimp and live within their means. Maybe they adopt the philosophy that if they do not have money in their pocket, then they do not have money for what they want to buy.

"Or maybe they think they were already in too deep and chose bankruptcy—either way, once they are debt-free, they still need a financial plan. They need to change the manner in which they spend money.

"If how they spent money in the past led them into deep financial trouble or bankruptcy, then they must now fight to maintain that economic independence. By returning to their old spending habits, what will be the result?"

One of the kitchen workers had a face tattoo, the other with one on his neck. The Oracle opened the doors and then stood off to the side. It's not typical for a truck driver to help unload the trailer, but I wondered if it might even be the law, being that it was a correctional facility.

"I suppose same habits, same debt—eventually?"

"It is my observation that once people become free of their financial problems, they breathe a sigh of relief—then immediately afterwards compensate for their struggles by returning to the spending game. They think, 'Now we can afford to buy that entertainment system we always wanted!'"

"That's grim."

"Debt is a life sentence. Most often they are back into the same amount of problems, or more than they were before within a few years."

"You make it sound hopeless."

"Life is hopeless." Tattoo face chimed in.

"You're right."

I only have one rule in life—always agree with somebody who has a face tattoo.

"For them, unfortunately, it is. You, however, do have hope. As you take control of your emotions within yourself, not only will it become apparent that most of what you desire is trying to fill empty emotions with material things—you'll also free yourself to create more wealth and use it towards what truly increases the joy in your life."

"That's deep," neck tattoo guy said as he rolled the loaded pallet jack into the building.

"That should be considered as one of the Baby Steps." I agreed.

"You're right—number twenty-seven!"

"Twenty-seven!"

Baby Step #28

"Wow, I can really see why some people want to be cattle ranchers." I took a taste of my brown sunshine.

After a long day's drive yesterday, we found ourselves in the heart of Texas waiting for a livestock trailer to be loaded with cattle. They couldn't load the trailer until we were ready to pick it up because cattle don't enjoy sitting around like that.

This morning, the Oracle volunteered me for his exercise program—at five in the morning. We walked across this open field to the only hill in sight, with nothing more than a flashlight and a cup of coffee.

I could not call it a mound, even though it was shaped somewhat like a pitcher's mound, but I couldn't call it a mountain because it was not tall enough. It was barely big enough to cause me to stop two or three times to catch my breath.

What made it difficult was that it was covered in medium-sized round rocks that broke loose with our every footstep. While this made it difficult to climb, considering both of us had a hand occupied by a coffee vessel, I had my mug and he had the King, we had some good fortune that there were some larger rocks on top to sit on.

While the sun cracked over the horizon and lit up the cattle farm below, it was almost hard to distinguish between heaven and earth.

"One thing is for sure, there are not many traffic jams out here." He twisted the cap off from the King and poured himself a cup.

"I can't imagine a greater lifestyle—waking up to a farm cooked meal along with a cup of coffee every morning. Then tending to the cattle and finishing the day off while watching the sun go down on the porch. It doesn't get much simpler than that."

"It depends on how you look at it."

"You're not going to tell me another story of hopelessness—are you?"

"It doesn't have to be that way. We choose how the story ends."

"All right—I have a warm cup of coffee, a good rock to sit on, and the sun is coming up. Bring it on."

"Number twenty-eight!" he yelled loud enough to wake up the cows below, if cows really slept. I have my suspicions.

"Twenty-eight!"

"Back in the mid-1800s, Henry David Thoreau wrote about sitting on a hill while watching a farm down below."

"Like this?" I used my mug to point down below.

"Precisely. He observed the cattle were trapped within the confines of the farm by the fence around the outskirts of the property. The cows could, for the most part, do what they wanted to do within these boundaries. When they wanted to eat, they ate. When they wanted to sleep, they slept.

"The farmer, however, could travel wherever he wanted—there was no fence for him. Even so, he had no time to go anywhere. He woke up before dawn, milked the cows, tended to the fields, and so on until dusk, when he would eat supper and go to bed.

"The farmer had no choice about his work because financial obligations controlled his life. If he did not take care of his farm, then the banker would foreclose on it. Thoreau asked, which is freer—the cattle or the farmer?" He finished the story with a drink of his coffee.

"You said that we get to choose on how the story ends, but does the farmer really have a choice? Doesn't he need to accept some obligations in order to start up the farm?"

"That might possibly be true. Perhaps without that pressure he would've never started in the first place and be stuck working for somebody else. Regardless of the why, aren't the results the same? Isn't he still a prisoner of his decisions?"

"I guess in this scenario I would say that it is the lesser of two evils?"

"Possibly. Let's think of it this way—we need money for many essential things… Our survival, which includes shelter and food, comfort, and freedom, to list a few.

"After we gain shelter and food, our first instinct is for comfort, but that is where we get stuck. Soon, what we once considered comfort is no longer good enough for us. Our house needs to be bigger—our cars need to be newer—our lawn needs to be greener.

"At what point do we say that we have enough comfort? What point do we say that we have exceeded true well-being and are buying things because of our need for emotional fulfillment or because of emotional lack?

"At what point do we say enough is enough—it is now time to buy our freedom? When is it time to stop buying bigger and better and start working on paying off our debtors? We do not deserve to be freer than the cattle, for we are not wiser than them."

"But you say that there is hope to be free?"

"Great hope," he said as he took another sip and went back to admiring the sunrise.

Chapter Eleven

"How long have you lived in Moab?" the Oracle asked Tour Guide Tina, the pleasant young lady we followed behind as we walked up the Onion Creek trail. I would say that she was probably the type of person who doesn't need caffeine—but drinks it anyway.

Rationally, I knew that he had days off from driving, but today, however, we found ourselves with a load from Denver, Colorado to Phoenix, Arizona and had enough time to stop along the way to do some micro-vacationing.

We chose Moab, Utah, as our first stop because it was directly en route and had plenty of open area to park the truck and trailer. Though, our parking still put us a couple of miles out of town. We signed up for a guided tour that offered free shuttles to and from our rig in order to see the area.

With millions of tourists visiting both Canyonlands and Arches national parks, we knew that those were not the places for us. Onion Creek was a well-known trail for off-road vehicles, but

Tour Guide Tina assured us it offered something spectacular for hikers, too. So far it was good, although I wouldn't say amazing.

The trail traveled through a small desert valley with sandstone cliff walls just high enough that a bird might need to take a couple of breaks trying to fly to the top.

The road was sometimes barely wide enough to get a vehicle through. That is, if we had driven one. It had a small creek running through it that contained sulfur which gave it the smell of onions.

It crossed through this creek almost thirty times. Each time you stepped into the water, your sandals would get wet and then immediately become balls of sand the minute you stepped out. I was sure that the texture of my feet had been completely worn off. The Oracle, not caring about impressions, wore socks with his sandals and, though the sand covered them, looked comfy.

Whatever this surprise was, had better hurry. The sun was hitting the horizon, and our shadows in front of us grew taller and taller. Though we had flashlights, I was hoping to see whatever this surprise was in the natural daylight. Besides, I assumed that being out in nature after dark would always somehow lead to a fistfight with an insomniac badger.

"I grew up here," she said.

That smile makes me want to belong to whatever mystical land it is that spans between her two ears.

"Bet you've seen a lot of change over the years," I commented.

"I have!" she said, again with that smile.

"Didn't this town used to be a lot smaller?"

"It did." This time with a small giggle.

"To think—back then, you probably had all these trails for your own. Do you enjoy all this new tourism?"

The Oracle looked over at me with a funny-looking smile of his own.

"No—no, I don't," she said, as if we were no longer friends. "Around here we call tourists desert fleas—they swarm nature like an infestation.

"It was nice back then. You could hike down the trail and enjoy the entire place to yourself. You could sit by a creek and peacefully enjoy the water go by. When pulling out on a street, you could turn left—you can't turn left now…"

"But isn't tourism good for the economy?" I reached down to loosen the straps on my sandals as the sand digging into my skin was becoming unbearable, then took a few big steps as to not break their hiking rhythm.

"But at what cost? What did we sell? And for what? So a few business owners could enter into the kingdom of the upper-middle-class?

"It's a simple case of supply and demand. When the demand increases, so does the supply. All they did was create themselves more competitors—and they sold our nature and serenity for it."

"I never thought of it that way." Realizing my error, I stopped again to tighten back up the straps.

"Then to see that empty dirt lot we used to ride our bicycles in as kids get ground up and turned into a condominium complex so some out-of-town investor can turn it into a nightly rental—everything's lost. There's no getting it back. Moab is dead to me."

Now is a good time to shut up—things are getting dark and I'm not only referring to the conversation, the sun is now halfway down. There is a concern about fighting angry badgers in the dark, but it sure is nice to have the heat starting to show mercy on us. Do they have badgers here? Of course—they must.

"Stop!" she suddenly pivoted around and shouted at us.

"What?" I noticeably jerked back.

"Turn around."

If I were a character in an old-fashioned comic book, I would have *gasp!* in my thought bubble. The desert is full of many mysteries that are hidden because everything is the same color, but when those colors change—things magically appear.

In front of the golden sunset on the horizon were silhouettes of darkened spires broken up by rays of sunlight beaming through them and the valley of the canyon. The once annoying creek now added a rhythmic ambience to the background. I once heard that God is an artist, but until now, I never really gave that much thought.

*

"Isn't that dangerous?" he asked her as she sat on the edge of the cliff with her legs kicked over.

The second part of the light show involved climbing up to the top of the cliff with nothing more than our flashlights to guide us, though it was not as dangerous as it sounds.

We did not scale up the side of the cliff wall as if we were goats with nothing more than a rope preventing us from our imminent death—no, it was as easy as continuing down the trail another half a mile and walking up where the four-wheel-drive road switchbacked to the top and then backtracking some.

"No—people don't die sitting on a cliff, silly," she said, returning to her usual chipper self. "They usually die when they hit the bottom."

"Reasonable argument," he sat the King on the ground and carefully flipped his legs over the ledge. "Come join us, Bud."

"I'm not sure how I feel about this."

"Chicken?" she asked.

"Chicken?"

I haven't got a clue how to answer that other than to join them. When a hyped-up chipmunk insults you, then there is no other option but to follow along or lose your dignity.

There was this feeling of the vast openness of the canyon in front of me and a mild warm breeze drifting up the cliff wall, not strong enough to move my hair, but more of a minute detail that I might only notice in the dark vacuum that is the desert at night. *This must be what floating in outer space is like.*

"Okay, are you guys ready for this?"

"For what?" I was already being on edge, literally.

"Turn off your flashlights and look up," she said as we all nearly simultaneously flipped off our lights.

Suddenly the sky shone with a billion stars. Once again, if I was an old-timey comic book hero, *gasp* would be in my thought bubble. What made it more impressive was that the spires off in the distance were silhouetted by these star sparkles.

"Wow, I think I can see to the outer boundaries of the universe."

"Echo!" he yelled into the canyon to see if it would resonate—only to be disappointed that it didn't.

"It's too small for an echo," she snickered.

Not being discouraged, he shouted out, "Number twenty-nine!" Still no echo.

"Twenty-nine!" she yelled—not wanting to be left out of a good time, even if she didn't know why.

"Bud, do you think you can jump to the other side of this valley?"

"Of course not."

"There is this moment in business that I call *jumping the gap.* Most people think that one moment they are working at their jobs and punching the time-clock, the next they are running a lucrative enterprise.

"But what about that gap in between? The gap in the beginning where they are suspended in midair? Where they are not making any money? Where they don't know if they will make it one more day?"

"Jumping the what?" I reached out to search for my mug in the dark, but then realized I forgot to bring it with me. This was a sure sign that I would be a bad trucker.

"It's no different from us sitting here and trying to jump to the other side. It's dark, terrifying, and you don't have a clue where the other ledge is at, the ledge where your operation supports itself and breaks a profit. All that you can do before taking this leap is to prepare the best you can."

"You mean save up money?"

"Among many, many other things—"

"Ooo… Sounds scary!" Tour Guide Tina chimed in.

Despite her mood swings, I like this girl.

Baby Step #30

"Well, I must say that this Baby Step is obvious." I looked over at the Oracle.

"Why do you say that?"

"The last lesson was about jumping the gap and, to illustrate that point, you took me to a canyon. Now, here we are standing on the North Rim of the Grand Canyon. Obviously, when you say that we need to jump the gap, you mean it is really, really, enormous."

"Then do you want to do the honors?"

"Of course," I took a deep breath in and with all my might yelled into the greatest void in existence, "number thirty!"

"Thirty!" His face showed excitement that this time it did indeed echo.

"Are you saying that all gaps are this enormous?"

"No, but some are. There are some that are relatively painless. Though, some take years to cross. It may even seem as if some are impossible. Every venture is unique and therefore every gap is different."

"What makes them different sizes?"

"Supply and demand, I suppose…" He paused and looked out over the canyon. "Maybe luck, too?"

"You don't sound too sure about that."

"I guess if anybody knew the answer to this question, then it wouldn't be very challenging, would it?

"I guess not?"

"Some are obvious, such as launching a motorcycle shop may have a sluggish start, but should experience a gradual increase if you're excellent at what you do. Life will be easier for you if you add great value to others.

"Sales jobs such as selling cars or real estate can be painfully hard. Sales people do actually add value to society—believe it or not. Car salespeople make cars available. Real estate agents help navigate the technical side of the sale. Even a furniture sales associate might guide you to the most comfortable couch to buy.

"The challenge with this enterprise is that the supply exceeds the demand. Sales people are the same as flies—for every one you swat, ten more land in your food."

"Isn't that the truth…" *Thankfully, this view sold itself.*

"This concept also goes for artistically skilled jobs, such as a musician, painter, or writer. It's hard to compete against an opponent who will do it for free, especially when there are hundreds of them fighting for a single spot."

"How do I equip myself for a gap when I have no idea of the size of it?"

"One thing I can say is that this is where deep research becomes valuable. The more you know about your market, competition, and your industry, the greater the chance you will be able to predict it.

"When you write your business plan, you might want to play it safe and plan for the possibility of delays or challenges. There is a lot at risk and you don't want to fail because of some unforeseen obstacles—do you?"

"I suppose, therefore, this is why my plan is so important?" Usually all of this would seem overwhelming, but the scenery really put things in proportion. The Grand Canyon had a way of making everything insignificant in comparison.

"Yes, of course. When trying to get a loan, the bank will want to see a solid plan. But it's essential even if it's not something that you're going to finance, such as starting a motorcycle shop in your parent's garage.

"A bank will also want to make sure you borrow more than enough money to get it off the ground. They know that if you run out of money before you bridge the gap, you will go bankrupt. Therefore, they will not see a dime of their investment again. They feel it's better that you borrow enough money for long-term success so you can definitely make payments in the future.

"Likewise, if you're planning on doing it with cash that you saved, make sure you have more than what you think you will need. Even with the most thorough research—the time and energy to span it cannot be accurately known."

"What should I do to ensure I succeed?"

"The rule of thumb that I use is—try to establish more than adequate capital with as little debt as possible. It's hard enough to break a profit without seeing your money vanish by paying on loans.

"Plan and save, sell the boat, get a night job, whatever it takes and even if you feel you have adequate capital, try to keep your start-up and running costs as low as possible—it's hard to say when you'll bridge the gap."

"What about just making sure I have enough credit limit on my cards in case I come up short?"

"That's a horrible idea. Never put yourself in a position where you need to use credit cards to keep moving forward. They can easily create a downward spiral that a weak business won't be able to survive."

"Got it. Grand Canyon good. Large gap unpredictable. Research good. Planning good. Debt bad. Overspending bad. Credit cards bad. Jumping the gap not good or bad, simply is what it is. Anything I'm leaving out?"

"Depth of understanding."

"What?" I looked over at him.

"We'll get to that later. For now, how about we take in the scenery and enjoy the day?"

"You're right, this place really put some perspective on how immense this planet is and how little we are. If only they sold fries here." My stomach was literally growling from too much brown sunshine and not enough food. I thought it would've adapted to the trucker lifestyle by now.

"Hungry? I know this great burger joint along the way."

"Let's roll. I can look at a hole in the ground anytime."

Baby Step #31

"We don't allow outside containers, sir," the young man commented about the King.

He was working the counter at Big Bob's Burger Barn and you could see on this kid's face that he only had this job because his stepdad forced him. To make things worse, his manager made him wear a name tag that said Junior. Hopefully, this was not his real name.

"It's okay—it's a registered emotional support service thermos," I defended the Oracle.

"Very well, then. Just don't let my boss catch you with it." He looked back, as if making sure his supervisor wasn't standing behind him. "What can I get for you gentlemen today?"

"I'd like to order the number seven pair-a-box combo," the Oracle said.

"Do you want to mega-size that?"

"I don't understand the question?"

"A bigger fry—would you be interested in a bigger fry with that?"

"Sure?" he said as if a car salesperson was trying to sell him on an extended car warranty.

"What is a pair-a-box combo?" I asked.

"Junior, would you like to answer that?"

"When Big Bob took his blonde mistress on a vacation down into Mexico, they came across a hamburger cart. After spending several minutes trying to get past the language barrier, the cook asked him, 'hambergesa con todo?'

"To his surprise, con todo means everything. The magical chef of this hamburger cart, as he would come to describe him, put on it a little dab of every single condiment on the cart. He said he had to sit on the curb and eat it with both hands as half of the contents fell to the ground.

"The pair-a-box burger is an adaptation of that concept. We start off with five all beef patties, then we go to the fridge and put a little bit of everything in there on it. Pickles? It goes on the burger. Bacon? It goes on the burger. Left over cake from an employee's birthday party? It goes on the burger.

"The pair-a-box burger is a truly glorious abomination of American excess. So much so that no average hamburger wrapper can contain it. It must come served in a shoe box."

"How does one come to eat one of these monstrosities?"

"There's no easy way, that's why we set up special seating for those who order it," he said as he pointed towards the back of the building.

"What the—" I turned around and did another comic book superhero inner *gasp*, but this time for all the wrong reasons.

The front of the restaurant looked the same as your stereotypical fast-food joint with earth tone colored laminate particleboard tables with molded plastic chairs, but it suddenly turned into small mint green tile that covered the floors, walls, and even the ceiling. At eye level were shower heads pointing straight out of the wall.

Below them were garden hoses with sprayer nozzles neatly wrapped around a reel. The table and benches were formed out of poured concrete and painted yellow. It resembled a combination of a prison cafeteria and an eighth-grade boys' locker room shower.

"Nice, isn't it?" the Oracle mentioned. "They added the shower head so the customers can wash their faces when they're done."

"Yeah, and the garden hoses allow us to spray out the area."

"I still have some questions, such as why do they call it a pair-a-box if there is only a single hamburger?"

"Would it be called an abomination of American excess if there were only one? Is that what you would like to order, also?"

"No, I'll just take a medium fry." I dug out some change in my pocket and started counting it. I still had some whole bills left, but were saving them for bigger purchases if needed. "Better make that a small fry."

"Let me buy your lunch," the Oracle offered.

"A man may have an empty pocket, an empty stomach, but is not empty as long as he has his pride."

"That sounds familiar—Socrates?"

"No, it was on a fortune cookie paper I found in your ashtray."

"At least let me offer you my fries. After eating these two burgers, I doubt I'll have the room—or the ambition to eat them."

"Those are acceptable terms, thank you."

*

"Thanks again for your fries."

"Are you sure you do not want one of these pair-a-burgers?"

The bottom half of the boxes were soaked in whatever was decomposing within. "No thanks, but would you care if I steal one of those lids to use as a tray?"

"Sure." Fast-food hamburgers rarely possess a strong smell—at least not the same as the small gust of warm air that insulted my nostrils when he broke the seal on that shoebox.

"Thanks," I said with a small cough. "Are you sure you're going to be able to finish both of those? Is that even a desire you have?"

"Of course not," he chuckled. "I've seen a lot of truckers eat a lot of things in my days, but I've never seen anybody finish the number seven combo."

"Then why did you get it?"

"So I could tell you about the pair-a-box dilemma."

"The pair-a-box dilemma?" I poured the fries onto the lid and proceeded to emptying the contents from the packets of ketchup and mayonnaise, swirling them together the best I could using a couple of fries.

"Yes, otherwise known as—number thirty-one!"

"Thirty-one!"

"There will come a day when Juniors friends no longer find it funny that he works at Big Bob's Burger Barn. People see him wearing a paper hat and they mock him. But that's okay because he now has his own name tag."   •

"There's nothing wrong with working at a fast-food joint. We all need to start somewhere."

"Fair point—though let's say that this young and ambitious man desires to own his own burger pit someday, but he says that starting any business requires a ton of money. He is barely making it day to day, so he stays there, stuck in a groove. That is the great pair-a-box."

"A what?"

"You know—pair-of-box. You should start building your enterprise when you're young, but when you're young, you don't own any money. The great pair-a-box."

"Ha! You mean paradox?"

"Yes, that's what I said, pair-a-box."

"Paradox?"

"Yes—pair-a-box."

"Continue then…" I said, dipping a fry in my home-made fry sauce.

"It is easier to be self-employed when you are young and have nothing to lose—it is more difficult to transfer from having a normal job that allowed you to buy large possessions and accumulate enormous debt.

"If you quit your normal job to set off on your own, it is almost imminent that you'll end up sacrificing some luxuries. It is easier to build a monument without having to watch old monuments crumbling. In other words, to build from nothing is easier than trying to hold on to everything that you own while building your future."

"You're saying that to start—the younger, the better?"

"If you have nothing to lose, then there's nothing to lose. Therefore, kids coming out of high school should only be employed momentarily while planning their future in self-employment.

"If they wait until they are in their late twenties, such as most entrepreneurs, they might own a house, car and maybe a boat, not to mention a family with eight hungry mouths to feed. They have a lot more that they risk losing. If he quits the Burger Barn now, all that he would have to lose is his old rusted-out van."

"What about the possibility of a lifetime of crippling debt?"

"Easy. Debt only comes when you borrow money. Don't borrow money, don't have crippling debt. It's as simple as that." He tried to wrap his hands around the contents of the box the best he could, but most of it remained as he lifted it.

"You're saying to launch with no money and no debt? And how is that supposed to look?"

"People start from nothing all the time. Start with what you possess and only grow at a natural pace. If you want bigger, work harder. It will come." Liquids from this truly grotesque atrocity ran down his forearms and dripped off of his elbows.

I would've lost my appetite if I had not been so hungry.

Chapter Twelve

Baby Step #32

"Is that a real missile?" I wondered how they would allow a civilian to come so close to one—not to mention transport it.

It measured about 45 feet long, and they painted it flat black. It was mounted pointing towards the cab of the semi. The camo green transport trailer looked as if it could raise the rocket to be launched at any location, given the necessity.

"I cannot affirm if it is. I cannot deny it isn't." Brigadier General Wonpact of the Southern Arizona Proving Grounds talked as if everything was a fact, even if it was not. "That information is classified, but I would recommend you drive cautiously."

"You trust him to haul it? I thought only military personnel had authorization for something like this?"

"Jimmy Z and I go way back."

"Way, way back…"

"Besides, he only has to make it thirty miles," he said with a laugh. "You boys in a hurry?"

"What do you have a mind?" the Oracle asked.

"We're fixing to drop some bombs on a boat we drug out into the desert. I've got a couple extra sets of field glasses if you're interested in seeing something get blown up."

"We have time," we both said at the same time.

*

"Easy there, kid. The planes are not even in the air yet and you're wearing out those field glasses."

"Why are you dropping bombs on a boat?" I continued to look through the binoculars.

"Meaning—why are we dropping bombs or why are we destroying a boat?"

"Both—I guess?"

"Well, kid, our jobs are to test and approve military equipment here. There is a pretty sizeable space between stuff being invented and being put into service—we fill that space. We're making sure those munitions go boom when they need to go boom."

"And why a boat?"

"There's an entire lake down the road plum full of abandoned old boats. It's like a landfill for poor decisions, but it gives us a bunch of excellent targets."

"Which brings us to—number thirty-two!" the Oracle shouted.

"Thirty-two!"

"So, you already own the boat and are unhappy with where you are at. Therefore, you decide to start off on your own. Realize that business is akin to fighting a war—there is a high risk of casualties. The boat might need to go."

"Boom!" the General added.

"Well, not quite like that. Let's say you are eight months into the first year of operation and you need money to pay your other debts—perhaps your house payment is behind. You have only a few options because the friends that you always borrow money from no longer answer their phones.

"You realize you must either sell the boat or go back to a normal job. If you do that, then everything you've been working towards will disintegrate. You'll need to start all over again after you get your bills caught up. That means totally beginning again on jumping the gap.

"Unfortunately, most people won't give it a second shot. They shot their dreams down because they couldn't part with a boat. These decisions separate the entrepreneurs from the people who work for them. And for what? Something that in the future will be worthy of nothing more than target practice?"

"That's what I said—boom!"

"You're asking people to sell what they worked so hard for?"

"Consider which is harder, working to obtain something or working to keep it? During hard times, when you are working harder to keep something, does it make sense to free yourself from it until a time when you can more easily afford it?

"The entrepreneur makes a decision and follows it through. They'll only start a war for a worthy cause. They stay focused. They will only choose battles that will ultimately lead to victory.

They could choose almost any battle and probably win—but all battles come with costs and casualties."

"Such as the boat?" I asked.

"Boom!"

"Such as whatever you're willing to lose before giving up or succeeding. If you want to win the battle quickly, then you must buy weapons—laptops, business cards, yard signs... Whatever you find useful in your industry. These weapons come at a cost and increase your casualties. Your boat may be a casualty. Your car may be a casualty."

"What about our friend Junior back at Bob's Burger Barn? He has nothing he can sell to get by on."

"General—what would you train soldiers to do in a scenario where they do not have a weapon?"

"Throw rocks. Bite. Whatever they needed to do."

"What about the people who don't think it's worth selling their luxuries in order to succeed?"

"You must choose your battles when fighting a war. You must consider that the war you're fighting will be worth it when dealing with a casualty like selling your boat. If it's not, then you never should've started fighting it."

"Binoculars up!" The General yelled as if we were to stand to attention. "Five... Four... Three... Two... One!"

BOOM!

𝓑𝒶𝒷𝓎 𝒮𝓉𝑒𝓹 #33

"We're all going to die!" Sergeant Lewis yelled in midair, only he was too late.

Before his feet touched the bottom of the dugout, the enemy opened fire and covered his body in red splatters resembling a morbid Jackson Pollock painting.

The enemy was charging.

With one hand on his gun, the General held up the other one in a fist to signal to the troops to hold their positions. I held my place as ordered, laying in the dirt, paralyzed with fear. Then he yelled—three, two, one, fire!

Our entire brigade popped their heads out of the hole and opened fire as if they were homicidal synchronized swimmers. Within minutes, we covered the entire other team in yellow paintball splatters. Victory was ours!

*

"Thanks for letting us play war with you all," I said to the General as we stripped off our dirty, however paintball free, uniforms.

"These aren't games, boy." He looked over at me seriously. "If those men don't learn how to fight, then in a few months there's going to be a whole lot of farmers' daughters that become widows."

"Oh," I muttered.

"I think what the General is trying to say is—number thirty-three!"

"Thirty-three!"

"How do you fight when you don't know what you're up against?"

"I'm not sure."

"General?"

He looked up from untying his boots. "Before you start a battle, send in a few of your troops to test the waters while the rest of your soldiers stay on secure ground. This allows you to gather information about your enemy—how many, their location, their weaponry, and so forth."

"When starting out, people tend to go all or nothing, which is the same as having all of your troops rush an enemy hiding in the dark.

"They leave their secure jobs and risk everything. One should ponder this move carefully. First, contemplate if this is the direction you should pursue before quitting your job. Then ask yourself—do I need to abandon my work to start in this field? If the answer is no to either of those questions, then dabble your toes to test the waters." He put a clean shirt on.

"Is it possible to start slowly?" I tried to wipe my face off with my dirty shirt, though I doubt it helped any.

"Several can be launched as part time, but, yes, it'll likely be painful. You may feel as if you're working three jobs—and it will most likely eventually require your full-time attention. Though you would be sure that this is what you want to do by testing the waters.

"Those that require a full commitment before testing them out—I advise you to research them thoroughly."

"You mean demographics and a business plan?"

Why were we changing clothes when we haven't had a shower yet? All that we are doing is making our clean clothes dirty.

"To start with. The more knowledge you possess, the more likely you'll succeed. Remember, seventy-five percent of businesses fail in the initial three years. Only one out of sixty real estate agents makes it past a year.

"I've seen many people start a profession only to find that it is not their calling. Dabbling your toes allows you to test the potential opportunities without losing too many troops. That being said—we have a missile to deliver."

Baby Step #34

"Where are we going?"

I was glad that we had dropped off the missile for many reasons, but one being that we were now running bobtail and the back roads of Yuma seemed too narrow for a trailer.

"I figured since we were only a few streets away from the racetrack, we should stop in."

"Racetrack? Really!" A smile came across my face large enough that it made me question if I had brushed my teeth well enough that morning.

"I'm serious. I wouldn't play around concerning a good day at the track."

Speed is speed. It doesn't matter to me what kind of event it is—cars or motorcycles.

"Tell me, bud—how did you learn how to ride motorcycles?"

"Well, my dad took me camping, put me on a motorcycle that was slightly too large for me, and let me annoy the other campers."

"Didn't that seem dangerous?"

"Not really. He never showed me how to take it out of first gear."

"Let's go back even further than that. Before you slung your leg over that motorcycle for the first time, how did you learn how to keep your balance? How did you figure out how to steer and brake?"

"I suppose from hopping on a bicycle as a kid and skinning my knees."

"Do you think you're now a good enough of a motorcyclist to race?"

"Maybe enough to show up and not embarrass myself."

If you don't consider last-place as an embarrassment.

"What would happen if you were competing with the rest of the crowd and you made a slight mistake that caused you to crash?"

"I've no idea… I suppose that there would suddenly be a rapid series of events that would ultimately end with a splat sound."

"Can we all agree that every great motorcyclist and strong competitor began with humble beginnings? Scraping their knees riding on their bicycles?"

"I guess so."

"I often hear people say that they want to run a successful mega-enterprise and compete with the best of them. They don't comprehend that any choice they make at that level might eventually end with a splat.

"It is in the gap of struggle where they may make poor decisions without great ramifications. It is here where they may tumble and only have to worry about scraped knees.

"The gap is tough and emotionally demanding, but we should embrace it because it allows the space to grow into the type of person who makes all the right decisions when they count—at full throttle."

"Embrace the gap?" I physically shuttered a bit, hopefully not enough to be noticed.

"The way you described your learning experience made me think of another thing. Imagine a novice entrepreneur musters up the courage to fling their leg over the bike and enter the track. They wind up the motor, dropped the clutch, and race down the straightaway—in first gear.

"It's exciting—the force of acceleration, the streaks of things flying past them, the sound of the motor revving up. But then that's it. They continue on, stuck in that one gear. Why?"

"Because things become scary after that."

"And so there they are, trying to jump the gap, stuck in the lowest gear."

"What do they do?"

"They can either keep struggling until they run out of gas, or upshift and go for it. Business is definitely an adrenaline sport. Sometimes you get the trophy, sometimes you get the big splat.

"I think it definitely depends upon how much experience you gain before you succeed. Like I said, embrace the gap. Your business might depend on it."

"Wait—where's the race track?" There was a full parking lot, but I didn't hear the sounds of the motors.

"This is it."

"It looks like a—is this a flea market?"

"They call it a swap meet here."

"But you said race track?"

"It is. This is the old track where they had the dog races and now it is a swap meet."

"But no cars? No motorcycles?"

"No, but they sell tacos. You haven't lived until you've had a swap meet taco."

"Fair argument, let's go."

Chapter Thirteen

Baby Step #35

"Imagine having to weld all of those pipes together," I mentioned as we pulled into the oil refinery.

Between all the buildings and tanks were large metal pipes in every direction—almost like a large bowl of spaghetti with a tiny bit of tetanus sprinkled on top.

"Sure is something."

"You know, a few weeks ago I would've been nervous about having a tanker full of jet fuel behind me, but after riding around with a missile only a few feet behind the back of my head—jet fuel doesn't seem that dangerous."

"Why are you saying that we're picking up jet fuel?"

"Call it a hunch… We're pulling into an oil refinery with an empty tanker trailer, and I'm only assuming it's jet fuel."

"Were picking up marbles."

"Marbles?"

"Yes, what's wrong with hauling them? They have to get to toy stores somehow."

"You're saying that we are going to fill up this tanker full of little glass balls?"

"Of course—if we used a box trailer, then they would roll around. Which would be dangerous."

"And these pipelines?"

"Full of marbles."

"Okay, I'll bite—number thirty-five!"

"Number what? Why do you think this is a Baby Step? Do you not imagine that we're picking them up?"

"No."

"Fine—number thirty-five!"

"I'm listening."

"Imagine you have a long lead pipe floating in the air and you are standing at one end of it. You put a marble inside the pipeline and nothing happens. You put another in it and still no results. So, you start frantically ramming them into it until it is full. Then one falls out of the other side. All of that effort merely to see a single marble come out the other end."

"Such as trying to fill one of these gas pipes, but with marbles?"

"Yes, however, now you have your pipeline full. For every one you put in, you get one back out the other end. I can't imagine a better way to look at business than this metaphor. You work hard and get little or no results—right when you are about to give up, you hear this little *plink* on the other end in the form of a small profit.

"Some ventures have longer pipelines than others and therefore may require more effort before you see any results.

Real estate is a brutal example of this. Most rookie real estate agents are considered lucky to see a sale in their first year, but some will ram it full and are off running in a few months."

"I can see how it could be brutal to break into—so many other associates you're competing against with more experience than you."

"Indeed, and some may have ones so long that it could take years of sweat and mental abuse before it pays off. It took decades for Truck Stop Tom to get to where he is now. However, Snow Queen Sally took off the first month and with basically nothing."

"I can see that—all she needed was a plow truck and a cup of hot coffee."

"Here's the real kicker—you spend months packing it full, solely trying to get something to come out on the other side. Then you turn your back for a second and you hear the *plink* on your side of the pipe. Your marbles are falling back out!"

"What? That's not part of the deal!"

"I learned this ironic little lesson when I first started driving truck. After spending months drumming up loads and creating rapport with potential clients, I then took a well-deserved vacation of two weeks at Lake Powell, during which there was hardly any place I could get my cell phone to work."

"It's hard to imagine there used to be so many places without cell service."

"That was a while back. I came back to see all my marbles lying on the floor. Distributors would go with different drivers. Previous clients would find other truckers to haul for them. It was the craziest thing to experience.

"Of course, trucking is like a swinging door, which is constantly in motion. I barely had time to unpack my swimsuit before I was driving again. But since then, I can understand why people neurotically keep an eye on their phone, even on their days off—and develop a nervous twitch on vacations."

"That sure seems like a problem."

"Another common tendency of entrepreneurs—they lack the focus on keeping it to a single project. They'll start one project over here, one project over there, and do a little something else on the side. They have two or more pipelines and they are trying to fill them all simultaneously.

"There are many problems which come from this. Most people struggle to fill a single pipeline, and they usually give up before they are even halfway there. By having many of them, the chance that they follow through on any of them greatly diminishes."

"Such as starting a motorcycle shop and perhaps simultaneously opening a dry cleaner, for instance, would be a bad idea?"

"Merely opening a motorcycle shop is a long pipeline that requires a lot of effort to see any results. Adding a dry cleaner to it would be absurd.

"Imagine starting the motorcycle shop pipe and then turning around, you fill your dry cleaner pipe. You grab more marbles only to hear a *plink* behind you. They are coming back out of the wrong end of the motorcycle shop pipe!

"You grab some more and frantically start putting them back in the pipe, but then you hear, *plink-plink-plink* coming from the other pipe!"

"I see your point."

"The point of this is that launching or operating numerous businesses at once is for a skilled master. We normal people will simply lose all of our marbles!"

"That was a pretty elaborate story only to say stay focused or you'll drive yourself nuts."

"Yup—pick one thing and you might just succeed at it, pick many things and fail at all of them."

Baby Step #36:

"Are farmers always late getting their trailers loaded?"

"If you're lucky," the Oracle said as he took another bite out of his cherry pie.

"We seem to be lucky a lot."

"There's a trick I've learned. When picking up a load from a farm, always be punctual. Sure, I could say if they are usually delayed, then why don't I arrive late, but if I show up promptly—I get cherry pie, possibly a cup of coffee. Maybe a sandwich or dinner? Always be on time." He leaned back in his chair.

We sat on the front porch gazing out at the good old-fashioned country entertainment—the rounding up of the chickens. Something I've learned through all these travels is that older men try to stick to bean farming, possibly hay if they have some teenage boys willing to toss the bales come harvest time, but chickens, those are for the children and they couldn't have been happier out chasing them than if it was somebody's birthday party.

While the children gathered up the chickens, the older farmers stood around and talked about whatever older farmers talk about. Their wives were inside giggling at whatever farmers wives giggle at—which was probably the farmers.

Back in college, there'd be some group which would complain about the archaic gender roles, but around here it is all they've ever known and it suits them fine. As for who cooked this cherry pie, they have my utmost respect.

"I could sure get used to the simple life," I said, taking a bite out of my slice of pie.

"What word would you use to define the opposite of the simple life?"

"I would say complexity."

"That's a good word to use. Describe it in your life back when you were at school."

"Well, I guess there were a bunch of things I'd have to juggle. I had my social life, studying, trying to get my money to stretch and other stuff."

"What about all the little things—like buying shoes or making sure your car runs?"

"Yeah—sure. I had those things."

"And what about washing dishes, doing laundry, throwing out old food from the refrigerator, taking out the trash, getting a haircut, putting gas in your car, and so on?"

"Yeah—I had all those things, too."

"How much more of it do you think you'll have when you get older?"

"I can't imagine—mowing the lawns on weekends, shuffling kids around, trying to make my boss happy. I'm going to enjoy being young for as long as I can." With the last bite, I stared at my fork, upset that it was over.

"But someday you will grow older and you might have that house with a lawn, three cars, a boat, and maybe, just maybe, a vacation house. All of this will require to be upkept, cleaned, painted, and so forth."

"All of that is something I don't even want to think about right now." I licked my finger and pulled up the crumbs on my plate.

"I hate to say this—a business is nothing more than a monster which feeds on complexity like it is its food. You will be constantly answering phone calls, driving to the store after paperclips, refilling the toner in the printer, and so on. The more you can feed this monster, the bigger it'll grow."

"That's an interesting way of looking at it."

"This is where people see things all wrong. In order to be successful in their eyes, they have to radiate that image. They buy the big house, the three cars, the boat, but at what price? They think it is only a financial one, something they may or may not afford easily, but they do not realize that it is also adding complexity to their lives."

"I cringe at the thought of having to sit down with my checkbook and pay those bills every month." I unashamedly leaned over and licked my plate.

"Take a glance at all these chickens running amok and consider them as some aspect of complexity. Maybe that one over there is getting stuck in traffic, maybe that one over there is putting your coffee mug back where it goes, maybe that one over there is a client you need to touch base with."

"Okay."

"Now realize that there are two types of chickens out there, personal or business complexity. Can you tell me which ones are which?"

"They all look the same to me." I peered up from my empty plate.

"Exactly, and that is how it behaves in our real lives. Personal and business complexity blend into the same pot and the more personal there is in it, the less room there is for the other. By having too much personal complexity in your life, you are choking your enterprise and preventing it from growing."

"You're saying that a simple personal life is actually critical for success in other areas?" I awkwardly stared over at his pie, which only had a single bite missing, and thought of how I could get the rest of it over onto my plate without him noticing.

"I'm saying to focus your complexity on where it needs to be. You only have so much of it to go around. Feed the monster." He tore into the pie like he was the monster.

Baby Step #37

"Wrangler Randy!" the Oracle said with excitement as the farmhand met us halfway across the dirt lot, which was the farm's entrance.

"Jimmy Z!" He quickly pulled off his worn leather glove to shake his hand.

We both brought a pair of our own gloves. Showing up on a farm without a pair of gloves is like showing up for a drag race without a car.

"This is Bud."

I quickly put on my gloves before shaking his hand.

"I'm Wrangler Randy—my friends call me Wrangler Randy."

"Good to meet you—um—Wrangler Randy. I'm Bud, the Oracle calls me Bud."

"Where do you want me to park so these can be unloaded?"

"Right there is fine," he said with a smile, as if he was truly happy for a visitor. "While my ranch hands unload that trailer, why don't I give Bud a tour of the farm?"

"That would be great," the Oracle agreed.

"Well, over there you have the farmhouse," he said, simply pointing at it. "Those buildings over there are buildings, and the chickens roam out there in a fenced in part of the field. That's about it. That's the farm."

"What goes on inside those buildings?"

"That's where we process the eggs and put them in cartons."

"Who picks up all the eggs out in the field?"

"Why the children, of course." He chuckled.

"Isn't there some kind of child labor laws?"

"Not on a farm, besides it's not really work for them. We just convince them every day is Easter."

"And they fall for it?" I wasn't sure if it was genius or cruel.

"Took me until I was fourteen to realize it wasn't."

"You've been in the chicken industry your whole life?"

"You don't become a professional chicken wrangler like myself unless you do."

"—and what does a professional chicken wrangler do?"

"Can I answer this?" the Oracle interrupted.

"Be my guest."

"Okay then—number thirty-seven!" He clapped his empty gloves together as if it was to stir excitement.

"Thirty-seven!"

"Thirty-seven!" Wrangler Randy joined along as if he was genuinely happy to be there.

"If paying our credit card bills, mowing our lawns, running little Bud to soccer practice, and pretty much everything else we do and mislabel as normal daily life is actually personal complexity," he put his gloves on, as if he was about to wrangle some chickens, "and if refilling the coffee pot, returning emails, returning phone calls, and everything we mislabel as normal daily work life is actually business complexity—then pretty much our entire lives, from the time we wake until we go to bed, is managing this monster."

"Yep, that's what I do," Wrangler Randy said as we both glared over at him.

"No matter how much we simplify our personal or business lives—there will still be this monster. And though they both may be different, they feed off from the same resources. Therefore, we must manage them as the same thing.

"If complexity was like a chicken, then an entrepreneur would be a professional chicken wrangler. They would have to make sure that the chickens which needed to be over there, were over there, the chickens which needed to be over here, were over here, and juggling six live chickens in midair all at once."

"I can do that." We looked over at him again, this time because we believed him.

"How you reduce the complexity in your life by simplifying, and how you manage the rest will determine how well you prosper. It is essential that you learn how to wrangle your chickens."

Chapter Fourteen

Baby Step #38

"Filling in your logbook?" I hopped into the Beast, threw my bag of plain potato chips onto the dash in front of me, and popped open my can of diet soda.

After being on the road for weeks with him I have adapted—my butt doesn't hurt as much from the coils in the seat, my spine is decompressing, I've learned to make an entire meal out of rest stop vending machines, and I've picked up a bit of the lingo.

A truck driver is only allowed to drive eleven of fourteen hours and then they must rest for ten. To keep track of that, they have logbooks that are inspected regularly at weigh stations or by curious police officers.

"Yeah—wait, no. It's similar to a logbook, but it's not." He pulled his attention from it and looked over at me. The dome light of the Beast was fairly bright, but still made reading and writing strenuous on the eyes.

"That makes no sense."

"Chips and soda? It must be dinnertime."

"It is." I took a sip of my diet cola. It wasn't as satisfying as a cup of brown sunshine, but the rest area didn't provide any coffee vending machines.

"You know what else it is time for?"

"No?"

"Number thirty-eight!"

"Thirty-eight!"

"One of the most important lessons which I've learned is that there is a fine line between being self-employed and unemployed. This even applies for long-haul drivers."

"Really?" I set my cola in the cup holder and opened my chips.

"Yes, because most self-employed people, including truck drivers, fail to put forth enough effort to be considered as employed. Although, if you accidentally call a hard-working self-employed person unemployed, you stand to get a black eye. The hard-working people often receive a bad rap from the truly unemployed—these two types of people shouldn't be confused."

"I understand how that can frustrate those who really do work hard. How do you know for certain which side of that line you're on?"

"Well, if you want to know whether you are self-employed or unemployed, take your day planner and rip all the pages out of it. Chances are, you probably won't need them to keep things under control. Personally, the most use I've seen from it is as a pillow when I need to take a snooze in a parking lot."

"I don't own a day planner." I popped a chip into my mouth, not realizing how loud it would crunch in the vacant night air.

"Step one, buy a day planner. Step two, tear out all the pages."

"Will do."

The potato chip, the fry's crispy cousin.

"Between truck driving and recruiting people for my MLM group, I prefer to keep my schedule busy, on the verge of thinking that I'm about to lose control. Yet, somehow, things stay together. At this frantic pace, who has the opportunity to fill in a schedule?

"If it's important, I'll write it in my notebook. In the mornings, I'll pour myself a cup a coffee and I try to envision what the day is going to look like and the things that I need to accomplish.

"I never know everything that it'll bring me—that's part of the excitement. At least by my morning reflection, I know which direction I'm traveling and when I'm supposed to get there."

"How do you keep honest with yourself? Perhaps you have a slow day, then another? How do you keep track of it to make sure that you're still moving forward?"

"Take a gander at this—" he said, showing me his writing pad, "instead of the day planner, I use this small three-ring binder. Inside, I have a sheet that resembles a punch card that has blank lines next to the times. When I shut my truck down for the night, I pull it out and I mark *in* and *out* for the moments I worked, driving and otherwise."

"Okay, that makes sense. If you are your own boss, that means that you are your own employee." I tossed in another chip and tried to chew it slowly, somehow thinking that it would be quieter.

Time Sheet	
8:00	in driving
9:00	
10:00	
11:00	
12:00	
1:00	
2:00	
3:00	
4:00	out driving
5:00	in exercise
6:00	out exercise
8:00	in MLM
11:00	out MLM

"That's one way to consider it. I thought I was putting in a lot of effort when I started using my work log. At the week's end, I was only working sixteen to twenty-four hours a week. I was barely grazing my butt above being considered unemployed. That explained many of the terrible results I was getting. Half of the battle is showing up."

"The hours do tend to slip away."

"After I pulled my hours up, I started focusing on how much of that was amateur work. How many needless stops am I making? Do I really need some beef jerky right now? How often am I taking lunch or making unnecessary phone calls? How often do I clean up after myself?"

"Some of those are important." I made another attempt at eating a chip. This time I thought I would suck it to make it softer before chewing.

"Are they? Over the years, my work log has become more sophisticated. When I have had many projects going simultaneously, I gave each project a two-letter code to go next to the 'in and outs' on the time sheet. This way, if a project was suffering, I could take a glance at the time sheet and see if it was getting the proper attention. This is marble management at its finest."

"Hark, those pesky marbles." I crushed the potato chip in my hand before putting it in my mouth.

"I added a code for doing push-ups in the parking lot or going for a jog and I count this time the same as if I was at the office. After my long hours of driving and recruiting, I noticed that I never had a chance for physical fitness.

"Having a healthy body is as essential as having a powerful mind. Nothing will be accomplished if you lack the energy to put into it. I feel it is very important to my success."

"That could be challenging." I looked at my bag of chips, wondering if there was any way to munch one that didn't make a noise.

"It is—therefore, for every hour I spend at the gym, I give myself two hours on my log. That way, at the end of a long day driving, I can tell myself I need the hours on it and I'll drag myself to put on my running shoes. Or in the weeks where I only have a few loads, I might make it up with lengthy power hikes."

"Yeah, about that—sorry for slowing you down." Frustrated, I crumpled up my bag of potato chips, turning the contents into salty potato dust, and then poured them into my mouth.

"No problem. I'll make up for it later. The point I'm trying to make is that I find the log much more productive than the day planner. After all, it's what you do, not what you plan to do, that leads to success."

"It's what I do, not what I plan to do? I'd almost feel as if I'm being attacked if I was the type of person to fill out schedules." By breaking them up, I let out the flavor crystals, so I tossed them back up on the dash and went back to my cola.

"Trust me, it makes all the difference."

Baby Step #39

"I'm not sure how you're not losing your mind right now. It is almost as if we are being attacked by these other drivers."

We were taking the traffic jam inch by inch. Whenever traffic moved ahead, by the split second he let out on the clutch, some car would dart in front of us and jam on their brakes.

After we unloaded the chickens, we were to meet another driver at a truck stop. He was to take our trailer and head back to Kansas. Unfortunately, he ran a couple of hours behind, putting us right smack in the middle of rush hour traffic as we passed through Denver. Luckily, this also put us without a trailer. I guess navigating rush hour could've been worse.

"Learn to be patient. It *is* as if we are being attacked by them. As if they let us move forward, we will only slow them down. But if we become angry, then it'll be like they are attacking us twice."

"That's a very enlightened way to take that."

"Besides, this is the greatest weakness of entrepreneurs."

"Traffic jams?"

"No, stress jams."

"I don't follow?"

"Often in business, and I mean often, we get flooded by stress—it swarms us like these cars until we are unable to move, leaving us completely stalled. This is particularly true when launching into the dark abyss of the gap—and especially if we are amateurs at it."

"What kind of stress are you talking about?"

The car behind us honked his horn, as if by doing that we would suddenly be able to move forward and let him get home ten minutes sooner.

"The stress of not having a safety net, the stress of approaching the deadline of when you're going to run out of money, the stress of transactions going bad, the list goes on and on. If you do not manage the stress, then it'll attach itself and render you useless.

"It might start off with watching TV a little extra in the morning, or playing on the internet. Soon you notice it's almost noon by the time you get going. Then slowly it may become later and later. Next thing you know, you're only getting a couple of hours of work done each day.

"Why go to work when there's only a couple of hours left before dark? It would be wasting your gas and resources. Maybe you'll just start early tomorrow. But tomorrow is the same, TV, internet, talking to people on the phone, and on and on.

"Next thing you know, it's been days or weeks since you've been working. Now the stress of that is overwhelming, crushing your soul, draining you of every bit of energy you've got left. You are literally frozen in place, waiting for the ominous moment you run out of money and are forced to return to the punch clock down at the factory."

"That's dark."

"That's real—very real. This may be hard to believe after the excitement of quitting your job and pursuing after your passion. Regardless of how passionate you are, nobody is immune to this. Nobody is safe. Not even the experts."

"Then what must be done?"

"You need to protect yourself from the stress. Take brief breaks throughout the day and breathe. Don't take things personal. Understand that bad things are a perfectly natural part of any endeavor, don't dwell on them.

"Also, prevent yourself from getting into a destructive groove—turn off the TV, unplug from the internet, distance yourself from all distractions regardless of your temporary addiction to them."

"What if doing that is only something they do until the caffeine soaks in? Or possibly doing it while eating breakfast? After all, what are they supposed to do when they eat? Stare at the wall?"

"Yes—in fact, they are supposed to stare at the wall. It only takes five minutes to go down a dark hole that consumes the entire day. That dark hole opens with the push of a single power button.

"Simply moving all those distracting activities to the evening might be all it takes to put motion back in our lives. But it's not that easy—is it?"

"It's a big request to expect people to not do that in the morning nowadays."

"That's because stress is pain and distractions allow us to unplug from it—even if it is merely checking our social media for a few minutes. But it might be the destruction of all things productive.

"Which is easier, turning off those devices in the morning, managing our daily stress, or spiraling into a clump of useless clay for months and months—until you run out of money and have to go back to work?"

He let the clutch halfway out before needing to push it back in quickly—yet another car shot the opening.

"That's still asking a lot…"

Baby Step #40

"There must be an accident up ahead." I broke the Oracle's concentration on the audiobook.

Sitting up high in a semi-truck allows you to gaze out over the horizon. However, traffic was stopped as far as I could see ahead of us, and the next off-ramp was at least half a mile away. We could always get off there and wait it out in a restaurant, that is, if traffic ever moved.

"I suppose so." He was unusually calm about the circumstance.

"I have a question—since it appears we have plenty of time to talk about it."

"Shoot." He reached over and turned off the audiobook.

"When someone gets stuck by allowing stress to get to them and everything seems hopeless… Bills are piling up, bankruptcy looms, and the threat of having to go back to the salt mines is imminent—how do they mentally get out of that and start moving forward again?"

"Anything specific on your mind?"

"Let's say I go out and rent a small shop area, perhaps barely big enough to work on a few motorcycles. Then a few months in, I need to juggle my bills—rent gets harder to pay every month, my phone only gets paid when they threaten to shut it off. Next thing I know, I don't want to go to the shop anymore. I find excuses to not work on the few motorcycles I have in. I stop prospecting for new customers. I am stuck. What do I do?"

"If you find yourself stuck motionless, the first thing is to redefine your expectations in order to take stress off of yourself. Perhaps you are demanding too much of yourself and, as a result, getting nothing at all.

"If we said to ourselves—today we must travel another ten miles, then we would add stress to ourselves. Obviously that next ten miles may not be possible at this moment."

"Less is more?"

"Second, try chunking the current demands into small actions and write them into lists. Choose a single item from the list, just one, and do it.

"I know I've ridiculed running after paperclips as a slow death to your business, but sometimes a small action such as that might get the blood flowing again and make the rest of the day productive towards relevant matters." He pushed the clutch in and put the Beast into first gear.

"What are you doing?"

"Third, ask yourself—if I cannot do what I feel I need to do today, what is it I can actually do right now?"

"What is it I can do right now, even if it is not what I think I need to be doing?"

"That is the most powerful question someone may ask under these circumstances. Mentally shut down? Run after some paperclips. Physically exhausted? Catch up on your computer work. Unable to physically go to work because there is eight feet of snow on the roads? Catch up on those professional calls you've been meaning to return." He spun his steering wheel and slowly let out the clutch.

"What the?" I put one arm on the door and the other on the dash to brace myself for impact, but somehow the front end cleared the car in front of us.

There is a crazy optical illusion that occurs in cab-over trucks. You can't see anything lower than the dash when it's nearby. If someone was standing a few feet in front of the bumper, you might only see the top of their hat.

It appeared as if the cab was crushing into the back seat of the car in front of us, yet it cleared and we pulled out onto the shoulder of the highway.

"Fourth, you may need to find an alternative path. Adapting is an essential skill of entrepreneurship. Just because you want something to go your way doesn't mean that is the way it is. We must be constantly ever-changing and moving with the flow of things. Don't let your vision of how things are supposed to be result in you failing." He started grabbing gears and speeding up.

"Okay," I said, realizing that bracing myself actually was a good idea.

His side of the Beast was still up on the concrete of the highway, but mine was in the dirt, which tested the integrity of the coil springs in my seat.

"Fifth, keep progressing—in any way possible," he said as we finally reached the off-ramp. "Even if it means moving slowly up side roads through the city. Take it one stoplight at a time and stay in motion."

"I heard you loud and clear on that." I took a deep breath and leaned back in my chair.

Baby Step #41

"When running your operation, tell me something you're not willing to do?" the Oracle asked.

"What do you mean?"

He pulled the Beast forward after unhooking the trailer and I felt the backend of the truck pop up ever so slightly. It is important to leave the trailer down a couple of inches when unhooking it. That way, when backing up to hook up, you're able to feel the trailer when it hits the plate.

The distribution warehouse was about the same as most of the others I've seen on this trip—a large old metal building with a couple of concrete loading docks off to the side.

Their yards were usually fairly large, about the size of a grocery store parking lot, and always had a couple of semi-trucks and trailers scattered about. Tall chain-link fences with barbed wire coiled up at the top always surrounded them.

"Tell me some rules you are not willing to violate in order to succeed."

"I guess I would prefer to not work Sundays."

"Why not?"

"That is when all the good stuff happens—barbecues, fishing trips, and such."

As we pulled around the building, we noticed that someone had accidentally locked the gate, trapping us inside. We got here right before they closed because of the traffic, but I would've thought that they would've checked to make sure the yard was clear before they locked up.

"What are we going to do?" I asked with a little crack in my voice.

"I think there's another gate on the south side," he let the clutch back out and hot rodded it back around the building. "Tell me something else you're not willing to do."

"I suppose miss out on important family events, like when we all go to the amusement park or throw family reunions."

As we pulled around to the south side of the building, we realized that there was no gate.

"Now what?"

"I wonder if the other gate was on the east side," he floored it once more. "Tell me another thing."

"Well… I guess I don't want to work too late every day. After all, I enjoy a good wind down in the evening."

As we rounded the east side, again no gate.

"Maybe it was on the west side? Tell me something more."

Didn't we see the west side a second ago?

"Overall, I don't want to work a lot of hours. I know video games sound stupid to some people, but I really enjoy them and would like to set aside some time for that."

"Dang, no gate on the west side either."

"What are we going to do?"

"Sleep here tonight."

"Really?"

"Uncomfortable feeling, isn't it?" He popped the brakes and turned off the motor. Suppose this was as good as spot as any.

"Very much so."

"Think of it this way—for everything that you're not willing to do, it is as if you put up a fence. Four fences and suddenly you're trapped within a box. What if success was on the outside of it? What if you doomed yourself to fail simply because of your unwillingness to be adaptable?"

"I suppose that too would be uncomfortable."

"Many people regard business as an opportunity to work a flexible schedule. Suddenly they have freedom, suddenly they no longer have to punch the time clock. But are they free? Ha! Not likely. It is very demanding.

"What I can say for sure is that you're going to be required to give up a lot of your video games, most of your barbecues and fishing trips, and possibly even a family reunion or two."

"Really?"

"You might also have to do a few things that you say you would never do, such as clean the bathrooms after it closes down for the night or scrub the grease off from the floors.

"The difference between a business and a hobby is that with a hobby, you may choose not to do the unpleasant things. I assure you that with a business, that is not an option. Every 'I won't' builds another barrier between you and success."

"I never considered any of that."

"How long would I last driving if I said that I refused to drive through traffic jams, up hills, or only wanted to work five hours a day?"

"I suppose that would appear to be a hobby."

"What if I refused to put fuel in my truck because I didn't fancy the way it smelled, lift the hood to check the oil, or crawl under my truck to put the snow chains on in a blizzard? How long do you think my clients would tolerate their late loads? Or worse, I decided to only drive them halfway because it was simply too far?"

"Wait—don't you take the winners off because you hate driving in the snow?"

"Not the point, but yes. Which brings up the point that perhaps your industry won't demand all those things from you. You might get nights free, ample opportunities to play your video games and make it to every fishing trip and barbecue, but you need to be prepared to effortlessly follow through on whatever the demands are that it asks of you. That is the true strength of an entrepreneur."

"Kind of like sleeping in the yard of a distributor because they locked you in—and not complaining about it?"

"Yep, this is just part of the deal."

Baby Step #42

"I never thought mirages were real." I wiped the sweat from my face with the bottom of my T-shirt.

A mishap in the scheduling put us driving directly through the center of Death Valley, California, at high noon. The antiquated air conditioning of the Beast was barely blowing cool air. The only thing that kept me from sliding off my chair was the friction created by my clothing.

It appeared as if way off in the distance there was a large pond and if we kept driving in a straight line, then we would eventually drive off into it, but that never happened. It stayed the same distance away as we kept getting closer. Although at this moment I would've welcomed the splash.

"It almost seems like a fake finish line, doesn't it?"

"It sure does."

"You know what else has a fake finish line?"

"What?"

"Business."

"How so?" I grabbed what was left of my thirty-two-ounce diet soda I bought that morning and took a big gulp—I didn't even mind that it seemed near boiling temperature.

"You have finally had enough of your boss and quit your job to jump the gap—"

"You mean the gap of seemingly infinite emptiness? The one where you have to eat noodles for every meal and pay for gas with pocket change just hoping that you make it to where you make a profit?"

"That's the gap, but where does that gap end? Where is the finish line? At what point does it make enough profit to sustain itself? We must be able to predict where that point is."

"Why? Won't we figure that out once the money rolls in?"

I grabbed my half-drunk bottle of water, thinking that it must have been better than the diet soda, but it seemed as if it was even hotter somehow. Instead of drinking it, I poured a little into my hair—only to have it run out and try to go down the back of my shirt. Although it was terminally soaked, too.

"Let's say that you're eight months into your project and are still firmly inside the gap. You've got three dollars left in your checking account, nothing but canned corn in your cupboards, and things are looking a little bleak. What do you do?

"The answer depends on where the finish line is at. If it is far away, you may have to make drastic actions—such as getting a night job. If the finish line is near, then you might be able to push through and struggle to the end. But what if it is a fake finish line? A finish line you keep chasing and never reach?"

"That sounds brutal." *But not as brutal as this heat.*

"Which brings us to—number forty-two!"

"Forty-two!"

"Launching a business requires desire. Running it requires logic, illogic, and perseverance. You need logic to make sound decisions. Remember, only you may steer the ship."

"I am its captain!"

"You need to be illogical to see past others 'logic' on what would be best for you. You know that their logic won't work for your situation.

"For instance, others' logic would be to jump to the safety of a standard job the first moment the boat is rocked. At the brink of success, they'll almost certainly still urge you to go back to a job and raise more capital—in reality, you know that will set you far behind."

"How so?"

"An unwatched business will go backwards. Then, when you leave that job, you'll have backtracked and are farther from success than ever before. That is, of course, if you ever leave the stability of a job again. After a long struggle, many cling to the security of the job even tighter than before.

"You need your own logic to know whether the finish line is fake or real. The danger of this is that wishful thinking often clouds your judgment on where the actual line is at. You might end up chasing after a mirage that keeps disappearing as you approach it."

"That sounds frustrating." I took my right shoe off and hung my foot out the window—my wet sock felt cool only for a minute, but it was worth it.

"It is, but if it is actually real, then you need to be okay with seeming illogical to others."

"That sounds logical."

"Finally, you need perseverance to see your decision through when things get tight and to hurdle you over the brink."

"Logic, illogic, and perseverance—sounds simple."

Baby Step #43

"Can I see your identification, sir?" the security guard who walked up behind me asked. He had a mustache—that was all that I needed to know of his character.

The Oracle who was sitting three slot machines down from me, broke into a fit of laughter.

After a grueling afternoon of driving through Death Valley, we thought we would spend the night at a casino in Las Vegas. Many casinos offer overnight parking for RVs and larger rigs, including semi-trucks. This is often the best accommodations a driver could wish for.

"I forgot it when I left home." I told the truth. Though getting carded wasn't uncommon for me. I had a baby face.

"Can you follow me?"

"Sure." I grabbed my remaining nickels out of the tray.

The Oracle casually grabbed his too and followed behind at a distance.

"Go ahead and wait out here." The security guard held the door open for me.

"Outside?"

"We prefer to think of it as a waiting room for minors." He smiled as he turned and walked away.

"That was funny!" the Oracle laughed as he leaned out the door. "Now come back inside."

"And risk me getting arrested?"

"I feel comfortable with that possibility."

"For what?"

"There's a free buffet we need to get in on."

"You mean free all-you-can-eat fries?"

"And probably more. They might even have some form of meat in there."

"Say no more…" With only a few steps into the casino, I saw Mr. Mustache had walked to the other side of the room. With any luck, I could sneak into the buffet unnoticed.

"What does gambling, finding a date, and opening a business all have in common?" The Oracle walked at more of a casual pace than I would've preferred. Perhaps his strategy was to blend in.

"You're sure to lose your money?"

"Ha! No, they are all a numbers game. Success is not guaranteed in any of them, no matter your skill level. Even the best players in baseball still strike out occasionally. And, yes, sometimes you lose your money."

"I figured as much."

The bright flickering lights and the sounds of ting, ting, ting from the slot machines surrounded us.

"These machines are easy to consider as a numbers game. Three of the five times you put a nickel in it, you'll lose. Therefore, it is almost certain that in the course of time, it will take away whatever you give it. That's why I only take two dollars with me when I go in. I consider it as paying for my overnight camping."

"That's quite the deal."

Mr. Mustache spotted me and we made eye contact. He immediately started our way as the hunt was on.

"It's the same as with dating and business—Perhaps you'll bear three failures and two wins."

"That's bleak," I tried to sound calm. "Perhaps we should walk faster."

"No, that's great." He ignored me and kept his nonchalant stride. "If you ask out five girls and three say no, that still means you get to go on two dates. Therefore, if you ask out one girl and she says no, then you simply need to ask out a few more. That goes the same for business.

"The sad fact is, half of small operations fail the first year. If you're part of the unfortunate half, then the odds are that the next attempt you make, you will succeed."

"What if I was really passionate about the project I was trying to start? What if there was nothing else I wanted to do?"

As we passed the blackjack dealer's, he was already next to the craps tables.

"With business, as with dating, you ultimately hold no control over whether it's a yes or no, whether you go home a success or you go home empty-handed. Sometimes you have to play the odds."

"If we're going to use that as a comparison—then what if this girl is my one and only?"

"If you ask a girl out, then she is the one who gets to accept or reject. Even if you think she is the only love for you. The best that you may do is buy her flowers and sweet talk a bit, but ultimately, it is her decision."

"And what if my business is my one and only? This is what I'm passionate about and no other will do?"

He was closing in quickly. I considered ditching the Oracle and making a mad dash.

"Likewise, you may try to influence the chance of success by working hard, staying focused, and perseverance, but it is up to the business gods to decide if it is a yes or no.

"That doesn't mean that you don't control a significant influence over the probable outcome, it just means that some ventures are destined not to succeed—at least not with the first attempt. If it is something you are truly passionate about and three out of five tries succeed, then if it was not this attempt—try again. The odds are in your favor the second time around."

"It seems as with all forms of gambling, you're always a second away from being kicked out the door."

The last step into the buffet, I jumped with both feet like a toddler—I was safe!

"Only when you're not accepted somewhere. As with dating and business, you'll know when you belong. With that being said—number forty-three!"

"Forty-three!" I turned and yelled at Mr. Mustache.

Chapter Fifteen

Baby Step #44

"Would you boys like another cup of iced tea?" The farmer's wife popped her head out of the screen door.

We found ourselves back at the Johnson farm for another load of hay, on time as usual, so we could reap the rewards of them running behind—a cup of ice-cold tea and some front porch sitting.

"Yes, ma'am," the Oracle replied.

"I'll be right back with it."

"Ma'am? Why is it that every time we visit the country folk, you suddenly get polite?" I asked.

"Around here you had better learn your manners, and I mean all of them. Ma'am, sir, taking your hat off indoors, waving to everybody who passes you on the road, regardless of if you know them. They'll forgive you if you forget to do one—but that doesn't mean they didn't notice."

"Here you boys go…"

I was sure it had been brewing on the windowsill for hours by how fast my ice cubes melted.

"Why don't you join us?" the Oracle asked.

"Don't mind if I do. After all, it is such a lovely day to be sitting on the porch."

"I don't believe we've caught your name?" He sipped some of his tea and gave out a weak smile, as if hiding how much he was enjoying it.

"They call me Bingo Betty." She put what was left of the pitcher on the small table between her chair and mine.

"That's an interesting name." I watched the condensation dripping off the side of my glass while I took some time to appreciate the moment.

"They call me that because I read the bingo down at the veterans hall every Wednesday."

"I'm Jimmy Z and this young guy is Bud." He took a big gulp of tea as his self-control wore thin. "Is there anything we should do to help get that trailer loaded?"

"Nothing much to do than watch. Those bales are too heavy to lift and we only have one old tractor."

"That still must be tough work. Have you ever thought about hiring a helping hand?"

"We did once, but never again." She theatrically threw her hands into the air.

"Why is that?"

"A while back, we hired this young man to work on this farm." Her gaze drifted off into the field. "He told my husband that he would work for a single penny the first day, two pennies the next day, four pennies the next day, and so on. Every day he worked—his pay doubled. They shook hands. You know, a farmer's agreement is stronger than any contract.

"Even though he started with earning barely a few cents, we had to fire him after thirty days. On day thirty, that boy made over five million, give or take a few pennies. Jim would've retired from farming years ago, but we are still working to pay that off."

"That really reminds me of something—" he stopped to take another swig.

"What's that?" I joined him on the drinking of tea.

"Number forty-four!"

"Forty-four!"

Bingo Betty didn't so much as flinch when we yelled it.

"That story is an excellent illustration of the concepts called compounding and leveraging. They are the core of investing in real estate. It allows you to double your money more efficiently than most any other investments. This is because of the highly leveraged, low down payment financing that is available for it. After all, investors are always looking for the best return for their investment.

"They may invest in a hundred-thousand-dollar opportunity with three grand out of their pocket. The other ninety-seven thousand comes via a loan. There are no other investments that can be financed to this extent."

"Yep." I was going along with the conversation, but really fixating on my tea.

"If you bought three grand worth of stock that was earning an amazing fifteen percent, which is rare, you would make about four hundred and fifty on your investment.

"Let's say that you invest your three grand on a hundred-thousand-dollar property that is appreciating at seven percent. You would make seven thousand on the same initial three-thousand-dollar investment.

"In three years, it would be worth one hundred twenty-two thousand five hundred. You sell it and invest your three grand plus your twenty-two thousand five hundred in profit toward a ten percent down payment on a quarter million-dollar property.

"It appreciates at the same seven percent, but that is now seventeen thousand five hundred you make your first year. Because of compounding, before long, your heavily financed three-thousand-dollar investment has made you millions. More people become millionaires by doing this than any other form of investing."

"If it's that simple, why isn't everybody doing it?"

"While this is the basic concept, there are a lot of considerations. Transaction fees might dwindle your investment quickly. When you consider that real estate agents, mortgage brokers, and title companies all charge a commission, you might easily pay your last year's profit toward transaction fees. This is not even including taxes."

"I'm young and while I believe I am smart—I know very little about this industry."

"If you're a casual investor, a mortgage officer is worth their weight in gold, a great tax consultant is mandatory, and a skilled real estate agent might be worth the commission if they are very knowledgeable in the market.

"If you are serious about this type of investing and such, it might be worth the effort to get your license and sell real estate for a few years to get your toes wet. During which, study market trends fanatically."

"Couldn't I consider the home that I live in an investment?" I chugged the remaining of my tea. My self-control hindered the slow enjoyment of it.

"Sort of, but not really as much as most people consider it. If you are paying more in interest on the mortgage than it is appreciating, you may very well be losing money.

"If you buy a house intending to live in it, I wouldn't consider it as an investment until you have owned it for many years. Wait until it has gone up in value and your mortgage balance has decreased. They say that in the first three years you live in a dwelling, you hardly break even because of transaction fees from when you buy and sell it."

"Then what makes a house an investment?"

"To make it a true investment, you need to have other people paying your mortgage interest—renting your property does this. While this is risky for many reasons, such as renters destroying the place or not paying rent, it is also very rewarding. Every month, your renter pays your mortgage interest while you reap the rewards of appreciation.

"In fact, they'll most likely pay your entire mortgage payment and put some money in your pocket. You won't have to use any of the twenty-two thousand five hundred of appreciation to pay the twenty-one grand in mortgage interest over the duration of your three-year ownership."

"So, you're saying to buy a house, but not to buy a house. I'm confused."

"Besides having renters and making it a real investment, home ownership still has benefits over being a renter. If you had high interest credit cards and car loans, you could save thousands by refinancing your home at a lower interest rate and paying them off."

"That makes sense."

Bingo Betty was still gazing off into the field and so I reached over and helped myself to another glass of iced tea.

"I would rather buy a property and rent it out to make money on it, then rent a cardboard box under the viaduct for myself. If you live in an apartment in the ghetto and you qualify for a mortgage, then you might consider buying something for an investment property while you remain living in the apartment. Even though people may look at you funny, it still might be a good move."

"That seems funny." I giggled awkwardly.

"Consider this—if you are able to receive twelve hundred a month from a rental property, and your apartment only costs four hundred a month, then you may want to wait until your money builds up. After that, you might be able to buy two houses before you decide to move out.

"You should always do a financial spreadsheet before investing in anything and as long as the numbers look good—it doesn't matter how logical it looks on the surface."

"Even if I do all the research, crunch the numbers, isn't investing in it still risky?" I was no longer drinking my tea like a gentleman—rather, more like a college freshman doing a keg stand.

"Definitely—there are two major downfalls of investing in it. The first is that high leverage financing leads to high returns, but it may equally lead to high losses.

"Even though it has an overall steady appreciation, I have seen market areas drop sixty percent over the period of a single year. If your hundred-thousand-dollar property was in that area and you sold it that year, you would take a sixty grand loss.

"In a recent recession, housing values dropped by an average of seventeen percent nationwide and, with many new homeowners only paying three percent as a down payment, they ended up owing more than their residence was worth. That fueled a huge foreclosure rate."

"Kind of like when a bunch of my college buddies had their cars repossessed because they owed more on them than they were worth and therefore couldn't sell them?"

"Exactly. The other downfall is that this type of investing is not very liquid." He quickly finished his glass and set it on the porch next to him. I had never seen him only drink one cup of anything.

"Liquid?"

"What that means is that if you invest money into it, then it is not easy to pull it back out. After you have made the investment, it could take months or years to sell. It would be very hard to get if you needed your cash for an emergency.

"Entrepreneurs may prefer leasing their building because leasing allows them to be flexible. Say that you take a loss when you're launching your operation. By renting, this allows you to downsize the building you are renting and frees up your money to keep things going."

"I see," I said, even though I really didn't.

"Let's look at it this way—if you own a gigantic structure to operate from, then you'll be locked into the current payments that now may be hard to afford. You may not need that size of a building currently and could take a loss because of it. This will jeopardize your success.

"On the flip side of the coin—by renting, it allows the business to move as it fluctuates. You might effortlessly slide into a more suitable location if profits soar.

"New ventures should consider staying fluid until things settle in. They may not know how much space they really need or the impact that the area will have on sales. You definitely do not want to tie up your capital.

"In the board game of investing, borrowing excessively could put you in a position where you are unable to fulfill possible future obligations. This creates vulnerability where you have to sell at a lower price, which jeopardizes your game."

"Okay, now I really do see. Real estate investing is good—unless it's not. Buying a building when you are starting out is bad—unless it's not. It all depends on how much risk you're willing to take, your financial resources, and your need to stay 'fluid.'"

I slowly reached over and filled my glass once more with what remained of the pitcher. The damage done to my bladder will be future Buds problem.

"Wow—that pretty much sums it up."

"Bingo!" Bingo Betty shouted as she broke her fixated mental state. "Sorry, I must've drifted off."

"That's okay—we've just been sitting here enjoying the weather."

"Would you boys like another glass of, oh—" she said as she looked at the empty pitcher.

Baby Step #45

"Here's your pass." The security guard of Freight Sailor Trucking handed the Oracle a small sheet of paper through his window. "It's only good for an hour, so don't make me come looking for you."

"Where do you want me to drop the trailer?"

"Stay to the right of the trucks going into the service bay. Turn left after you clear the building. Go all the way to the end and you'll see the trailers parked there. Then straight ahead there's a road that will bring you back out."

"Thanks," the Oracle said as he pulled forward.

"That guy was rude."

"They usually are. They don't like independent drivers dropping their trailers in their yards."

"What do they do in the service bay?" I asked as we drove past the long line of semi's waiting to get in.

It looked like a massive concrete garage with bay doors on both sides making a tunnel that the trucks could drive through. The greasy mechanics smudged the bottom section of the painted light gray garage while leaning against it and puffing on their cigarettes.

The entire yard used an impressive amount of concrete, stained from oil droppings and tire marks. Acres upon acres of nothing but old concrete.

"Everything they can. Almost all of those trucks in line waiting to get in have typically been out on the road for weeks with no maintenance. They need a team of mechanics to look over them when they come back in the yard and do whatever repairs they are able to get done within fifteen minutes."

"You mean like inspections, oil changes, and such?"

"And whatever else they can manage within the time. If one comes in with something broken and they can't repair it quickly, they shut it down for the day. Then they have to go to either the truck shop over there — the trailer shop over there — or the tire shop over there."

The buildings that he pointed out were all impressive themselves. Each of them, made of solid concrete of course, had between six and ten bays and was covered in grease marks exactly the same as the service bay.

"Wow, can you imagine making the payments on all of those rigs?"

The parking area became visible as we cleared the shops. They parked all the trucks to the right, all the trailers to the left. Whenever a driver entered the yard, they had to drop their trailer. Why? I don't know.

"Ha! Those are solely the unassigned trucks, or maybe drivers here for the night. All in all, this company has about two thousand rigs and three thousand trailers."

"That's impressive. Have you ever thought about buying another truck, hiring another driver, and expanding?"

"Of course—but it's riskier than most people think."

"How so?"

"That question brings us to number forty-five!"

"Forty-five!"

"Hiring employees is the same theory as leveraging your money to buy real estate, except that you are leveraging labor to run your operation. The key is to hire people who will make you more money than what you are paying them to be your employees."

"That seems obvious."

"It's not as simple as it seems. This also includes all the other expenses linked to a greater business activity—such as having to employ more secretaries or shippers, or having to acquire a bigger building and more workspace, such as buying some land and filling it full of concrete."

"So much concrete…"

I can't say for sure where concrete comes from, but I imagine that there's some massive open pit concrete mine that doubled in size when they made this place.

"Hiring employees might be the biggest mistake you make if you hire them before your business can support them financially or if they do not earn back what they cost. Since half of my enterprise is recruiting people for my MLM organization, which doesn't really pay well, I have to justify their existence from the trucking alone.

"I've tried hiring some people before, not drivers because that's a big step, but people to manage my amateur work—doing my billing, tracking my loads, that kind of stuff for my trucking and keeping track of my contacts, maintaining an email list and such for my MLM.

"My first half a dozen employees ended in a nightmare for me, not for them. None of them lasted long enough to train, and they knocked my operation back a few steps while losing money for me." He cranked the steering wheel hard.

It has always impressed me on how a trucker is able to execute a sharp ninety-degree turn and pull such a long trailer between others with only inches to spare as if it was effortless.

"Then did you go back to doing all that stuff yourself?"

"No, I'm much too busy for that stuff now. I hired Snow Queen Sally's daughter to do it for me. It's awesome, it's mostly all done by computer these days and so she is capable of doing it from a college dormitory. It only takes a few hours a week, and the money helps with her tuition."

"That's brilliant. That way, you don't have to worry about anyone wanting to be full time."

"Let's get this trailer unhooked," he said as he popped the air brakes.

The Oracle's Golden Step

Baby Step #46:

"We need to hurry and get to a truck stop. According to my logbook, I'm almost out of hours." The Oracle slammed shut the day planner looking booklet and tossed it on the dashboard. Space in the Beast was very limited and so it had to double as a shelf.

He thought he'd better update his logbook after unhooking the trailer at Freight Sailor Trucking. We started unusually early today and even though the sun was only started going down, we had driven too much for one day, by law.

"Have you ever thought about hiring another driver and sharing the same truck? That way, they could take over driving for a while if you run out of drive time?"

"You mean driving team?"

"I guess. It just makes sense to me. Between two drivers, you would never have to shut the truck off legally."

"True, but that's usually for married people or rookies."

"Why rookies?" This broke my attention from the sunset.

"Bringing on partners is a mistake often made by people who are afraid to run things on their own, not because they are busy and simply need more hands—which are usually rookies.

"I see new truckers try to partner up with another driver for any cause that they can think of, but it usually comes down to the fact that they are simply afraid of doing it alone."

"Really?" The sunset show distracted me once again. Not that it was like watching it go down over the ocean while sitting on a pier, but watching it go down over a trucking company had its own type of majesticness.

240

"This is also especially true in real estate. New agents feel like they won't be able to handle what is involved in transactions, but if they think it's hard when they only sell a single sale a year, wait until they have to split that check in two."

"But won't there be twice as many checks?"

"Not likely. It usually turns out to be two people doing half the work. I have only seen a few successful real estate partnerships or driving teams. I've seen it a million times and rarely is it a good idea."

"You said rarely?"

"It works sometimes, most often as married couples. Sometimes it's a project that requires a partner because of its scope. Sometimes it's rookies that are not good enough to survive on their own, but pull it off together. I'm not saying it doesn't happen—I'm merely saying it's usually a terrible idea."

"Let's say that I want to start a motorcycle shop with my friend because it sounds fun. How can that be a bad idea? Two buddies hanging out, working on motorcycles, telling dirty jokes?"

Ever since junior high, it seemed like any time that me or one of my buddies worked on our motorcycles, it was a group activity often lasting late into the night. Those were good times.

"Never ever, never, never ever, ever, do business with family or friends. The challenges and stress of it can, or almost definitely will, destroy all relationships, including marriages, siblings, and best buds."

"But what if I actually am afraid to go it alone?"

Though the question sounds like it's metaphorical, there is still some truth to it—maybe a lot of truth to it.

"Well, acknowledging it is the first step. There are many entrepreneurs that hitch up to any partner that shows interest, but is that best for you and your business?

"Rookies use every excuse under the sun on why it is a good idea. They can make better decisions by admitting it is fear. Starting out is scary. There's nothing wrong with being afraid, but don't let that fear lead you into poor decisions.

"Courage is not avoiding fear. It is doing what it takes to move your business forward—regardless of it. That being said, I'm afraid I'm out of hours for the day." He fired up the Beast. "We need to get moving."

Chapter

Sixteen

Baby Step #47

"I wonder what the holdup is?" I asked the Oracle.

We were the fourth truck in line at the guard shack of Freight Sailor Trucking, but the line hadn't moved for some time and the automatic outside lights on the shops were turning on. I could see him fidgeting. Running out of hours was a serious deal.

"There's a lot the guard has to check. He has to make sure that the driver picks up the right trailer, his paperwork is in order, and other things. There might be a discrepancy they're dealing with."

"What time do all those mechanic shops close up for the day?"

"The service bay is open twenty-four hours a day and never closes for any reason, since it's the entrance to the yard. The truck shop for heavy repairs, trailer shop, and tire shop will also most likely be open twenty-four hours a day, considering the size of the company. They don't want their rigs sitting because of a flat tire.

"There might be some specialty mechanics such as the person who does the alignments or takes care of the body damage and repainting that may do a normal nine-to-five shift. Then you've got all the staff over in the big glass building. Some of them go throughout the night, too."

"Like who?"

The bobtail in front of us popped his brakes and shut off his motor.

"Mainly dispatchers. The rest of the employees, such as billing or human resources, typically go home at normal hours. Mostly, the trucking industry never sleeps."

"To think of owning a company large enough to support a human resources department that does nothing but hire and fire personnel. How many people do you suppose there are here?"

"Well, besides the two thousand or so drivers, I would say a few hundred suit wearers inside that glass building, probably fifty mechanics in the service bay and a dozen mechanics in each of the other shops."

"That is a massive operation to run."

The Oracle agreed on the decision made by the rig in front of us and shut off our motor.

"Every entrepreneur must assemble a team, of sorts—even if they are not directly working for them.

"How so?"

"How so—number forty-seven!"

"Forty-seven!"

"Eventually you will require a team of professionals, no matter what your industry is. This could be a team of assistants, or of colleagues in your field or other areas that your business relies on. A restaurant needs a slew of distributors. A real estate agent needs a cornucopia of professionals.

"Whatever your profession is, there will be professionals you collaborate with regularly. Choosing these members is as important as choosing the individuals you hire. They'll make you either very successful or very broke."

"How do I build a good team?"

Suddenly, the line moved. We fired back up the Beast, pulled forward ten feet, and stop once more.

"Never be afraid of working with individuals smarter than you. They reflect your strength to your clients or customers. An entrepreneur usually majors in minor things. They rarely have fancy college degrees, but they hire specialists that do in order to manage all the tasks they know little about. While an entrepreneur may not know every detail of their operation, they can assemble a very powerful squad."

"And you say I can do this without having anyone punch a time clock?"

"When assembling this crew, there are three choices of employment you need to consider—employed, self-employed, and commissioned. There are advantages to all three.

"Hiring regular employees allows you to maintain more control over their schedule and performance. For something that calls for a reliable work force, for example Freight Sailor Trucking, this is typically the best choice."

"That seems like a big step."

"It is, and when you're first starting out, you may not be able to afford this luxury. By hiring self-employed, it may save you from many of the expenses of a regular staff. It saves you paying some taxes and benefits, such as medical insurance, because these are usually their responsibility.

"Also, when times are slow, it saves you the expense of a set payroll. They only get paid by the job or by commission only. The downside of this is that they are very unpredictable in their labor habits. If things get too slow, you may show up to find an empty office."

"That would be a surprise."

Thinking that it might've been a false start, he turned off the motor again.

"Then there are partial-commissioned employees. They hire them on a full-time basis, but only give them a partial salary and they earn the rest through commission. A prime example of this is waiters and waitresses. They get paid a small salary and earn the rest in tips.

"This allows the restaurant owner to fully employ and schedule them the same as traditional staff. They are required to work a regular schedule regardless of the amount of business and also save the owner's money on slow days."

"That doesn't seem fair."

The line moved again and, being wrong about the false start, he had to hurry and crank up the Beast as to not hold up the traffic behind us.

"You're right. Commissioned is the fairest for both sides and is usually the best way to build a team. They'll usually grind harder and complain less because they only get paid if they accomplish something. This system has a natural way of eliminating the weak links while justly compensating the strong."

"That seems to be the best option. Why are not all personnel commissioned?"

"It has its limitations, such as it is project based. You pay them to perform a task to completion, and that assignment requires a beginning and an end. If they must show up every day to answer phones, then they must punch a time clock."

"How do you find qualified individuals?"

The line was moving smoothly now—at least about the same pace as you would expect from the drive-through of a fast-food joint.

"The key is to find people who love what they do. Even if their qualifications are slightly underdeveloped, over time they'll grow and exceed your expectations. However, someone who has the qualifications but not the love won't be in the industry long enough to impress you."

As we passed the guard shack, the guard waved us through. No smile or anything.

"The security guard doesn't love what he does, obviously."

"Sometimes you need to hire the grumpy people, too."

Baby Step #48

"Crazy Carl!" the Oracle said as we walked into one of the back offices of Crazy Carl's Couches.

"My good friend, Jimmy Z!" He stood up and walked around his desk to shake the Oracle's hand. I stood a few feet back with my hands in my pockets.

Crazy Carl had on a baby blue suit with an orange dress shirt that was last in style in 1981. He had curly hair barely long enough that it looked like a briar patch—and it would not surprise me if a rabbit lived in there.

In fact, the entire facility looked peculiar. They tied so many balloons to the couches out on the showroom floor it looked as if a gumball machine exploded and somehow the gumballs were suspended in midair.

On the right-hand side of his office was a desk with piles upon piles of papers. On the left-hand side was a table of curious objects for a furniture store—a blow horn, a cowbell, and a pair of cymbals, among other things.

"We have a trailer backed up to the dock plum full of gigantic boxes. I would say they are couches or affordable housing units."

"If they are affordable housing units, then I'm sure I've slept in worse back when I was in college."

"Ha! Do you have some dockworkers that can unload them?"

"You know the drill." He smiled.

"Do you mind if I let my young associate, Bud, do the honors?"

"Only if he can do it with enthusiasm."

"Do what with enthusiasm?"

The Oracle pointed towards the table, "You see the mega-phone there—"

"The megaphone is for crazy sales," Crazy Carl interrupted.

"What's a crazy sale?" I pulled my hands out of my pockets.

"Anytime I see a young couple looking at a lamp, ponder, and then walk away, I run out of my office with this megaphone, push this button which is a siren to get their attention and then I say something like, 'for the next ten minutes all lamps are thirty percent off!'"

"Then how do we call the dock laborers?"

"Bud, you are going to need to grab the cymbals and run around the showroom floor banging them as loud as you can."

That seems odd.

"Isn't there an intercom system to use instead?"

"Never underestimate the power of good PR skills." He winked and shot me with an imaginary finger gun.

"PR skills?"

"Personal rapport, or the relationship you develop with your clients and other associates. It will assist you in all areas of your operation. Take into consideration—my customers are coming in to fill a need in their lives. Sometimes it's an emotional need, but I'm not here to judge. I'm here to offer them a better experience.

"When they come into my showroom, I don't want them to be attacked by a gangly bunch of salesmen trying to make a sales quota, I want them to be greeted by joyful humans who enjoy their job and are having fun—oh, and by the way, they also sell couches.

"These salespeople can't fake happiness—they're salespeople, not actors. I must constantly compliment them on a good job. Buy them donuts. Run up and down the office screaming 'Yahoo!' and passing out balloons. It doesn't take much effort on my part, but it is very rewarding for them to know that they are doing well."

"How do I develop my public relations skills? Is it all simply running around, clanking musical instruments in the air, and screaming?"

"There are many elements—such as strong communication, looking for the opportunity to praise others, and directing the negative energy away while sending positivity down the line. The stress of this place starts at the top and stays at the top—with me."

"You're saying that you can't express what you're going through on days that are tough?"

"Not necessarily that. You can be expressive. Just don't send it forward. When you're having a bad day, take a deep breath, remain calm and focused. By being stressed, you bring stress to others. There is rarely a need for tension. A person's primal instinct during a stressful situation is to fight or flight. They will either resist you or find another job.

"Either way, creating tension hurts their productivity in the long run. They'll pass your stress onto the customer, which hurts your sales even more.

"Bad day? Smile anyhow. Ask them how they are doing. Show your concern for them and let them know you are also concerned for the business. Then praise them on the good job that they've done in the past. Always leave a conversation on a positive note."

"What if they are the cause of your stress?" I walked over and picked up the cymbals.

"Remember to be respectful and professional. It's never a good idea to talk to a team member or customer in a way as a parent would to a child. Never talk down to them. Don't raise your tone. You do not need to bolster your ego by acting superior. This is a common mistake by bosses.

"All communication should be that of one adult talking to another. You need to treat them as equals. They are trying to make it through life the best way they know how, too."

"What about when times are good? Do you give them bonuses or anything?"

"I do like to praise my fellow associates, including the dock-hands and other critical team members, but admiration doesn't always need to be expensive bonuses. At the end of the shift, the top salesman gets to do a lap around the showroom, banging something loud and yelling, 'I'm number one!'

"And sometimes I might buy a cake and throw a party on their lunch break or throw an occasional barbecue. It is simply showing them I am grateful for all that they do."

"I never really considered all of this as part of running the show." I had never held cymbals before.

"It's almost critical. By letting everyone know you appreciate them, you'll increase the loyalty of them."

I feel the part of me that is a four-year-old noisemaker suddenly coming alive... Must not succumb to temptation.

"That's accurate," the Oracle chimed in. "I know a driver who worked for a company for three years without pay because the company was having hard times. They had taken care of him in the past and was merely returning the favor. When the company was back up on its feet, they compensated him by giving him a semi-truck worth triple what he would've earned in those three years. That's a true story."

"Really?" I smacked the cymbals together as hard as I could—you know, just to test them out.

Baby Step #49

"Crazy Carl, this is quite some operation you have here. Do you mind if I ask how big of staff you employ?" I asked.

We stood at the dock watching two enormous men unloading the new furniture. Even though they could unload some of it with the furniture dolly, some of it, such as the couches, were much too big for it and had to be carried.

"Not at all, let's see—I typically have fifteen to eighteen salespeople, they're the bread and butter, then you have the essential staff, dockhands, Suzie in payroll, the greeters, customer service, I would say about twenty-five to thirty at any given time."

"Wow, I would've never guessed that many."

"Well, we are open six days a week. Therefore, it requires duplicates of many of the positions."

"How many supervisors and managers are there?"

"None, I don't believe in them."

That's insane. How can there be no bosses to make sure everyone is doing what they are supposed to?

"What?" I looked over at him.

"I do it myself."

"How? You have piles and piles of paperwork on your desk to deal with, not to mention all the other things of owning a place like this. How do you find the time?"

"It might be about recruiting the right individuals, which is true. Maybe it's because most of my salespeople are commission, which is also true. I pay them a small base salary, but if they try to live on it alone, then they would suffer a slow, painful death. But I will say ultimately it is by creating loyalty with them.

"If I'm the one forcing them to knuckle down, they'll slack off whenever I turn my head. So, the best way to have them produce consistent results is by *them* wanting to work hard. If there is a bond of mutual respect and loyalty, then most people will feel good by trying to please each other."

That sounds crazy. How is this place not a complete madhouse under this philosophy?

"How do you get somebody to volunteer to do that?"

"Again, it comes down to hiring the right individuals. Although, what it mostly comes down to is that they want you to succeed. They want to feel as if they are part of building something. They want to know that they are helping an underdog, someone exactly the same as them, reach for something better."

"How can you do this and still be their boss?"

"First, by respecting them. Second, by understanding. And third, strong communication skills. If there is a problem with them or their performance, then you must be able to guide them to that realization without criticizing and, yes, sometimes you have to fire them, but even that can be done with respect and understanding."

"Anything you would like to add?" I looked over at the Oracle.

"Yes—number forty-nine!"

"Number forty-nine!"

"You have responsibilities of your own that you need to deal with. Your team needs to perform optimally, even when you are not supervising them."

"Yup," Crazy Carl agreed.

Chapter

Seventeen

Baby Step #50

"This was a great idea, taking a few days off and renting a fishing boat before I go back and begin my life," I said as I squeezed artificial white cheese onto my hook.

"Yeah, I just wish we could find some water to fish in." He was making himself a bologna sandwich instead of preparing his fishing pole.

"Yeah—" I glanced up at him, "Wait, we're floating in the middle of a lake."

"Are we?"

"Of course, you only need to look out in any direction to see it."

"Well, there's not any water in the boat, so there must not be any water."

"I don't follow."

"Perhaps you can follow this—number fifty!"

"Fifty!"

"There may be many reasons you don't possess the amount of money you would like. Your problems are not caused simply because you lack a desired amount. They are rooted deep within you."

"How so?" I flung my hook into the lake and pulled the tension out of the line.

"Poverty in this nation is a mental condition. This world is abundant with wealth. Are those who lack it conditioned not to see it? Are we not floating on an ocean of affluence? And yet they stare inside their vessel and say, *there's no money in my boat.*

"It's as simple as reaching over the side and grabbing some, yet they are so conditioned by their beliefs that they are only worth so much. They use negative thoughts to keep themselves down, and when they look down, all that they see is the bottom of the boat."

"I don't believe it's that simple." I slowly started rolling my line in.

Sitting there motionless and watching a fishing pole for hours is for old folks.

"They offer you five dollars to mow their lawn, but your car is broken. So, you reply you can't. In reality, there are many ways to accomplish the task. So, you can mow their lawn, but you choose not to put out the required effort to take a cab or ride a bicycle.

"If they offered you a million dollars, then would it be possible for you to find the way to travel? Now that they've motivated you? Would it be more accurate to say that you choose not to do something, rather than you can't? After all, there's always a way when we have enough motivation."

"I'd say that being a C.E.O. of a corporation or walking on the moon if I only desired it enough would also be inaccurate." I lost my cheese, so I dug the container back out of my tackle box.

"Would it be? If any human has accomplished it, then that means it's possible. What you are saying is that you choose not to do what is required to achieve those opportunities.

"To say that you can't do something could become mentally damaging. By constantly saying that you can't do something, the unconscious must follow those orders."

"Dang—not the unconscious again." With a swing that would make any professional fisherman jealous, I launched my fish killer nearly out of sight.

"Also, never complain about not having enough money. Never criticize those that do. It's not that they were born with a gift, and it's not because the world is out to get you.

"Complaining can program your mind to not be successful. After all, if you dislike wealthy people, then when you finally find great wealth, you would dislike yourself. The unconscious will play it safe by keeping you poor and likable. This is the psychology of business. Success breeds more success—if you don't have any previous success, you had better watch those that do."

"What about the well-off who really are jerks?" Slowly reeling the line in again, it got snagged on what must've been an underwater tree limb. This wasn't a man-made reservoir that was groomed before they filled it with water. Nobody knows what kind of vegetation, old cars, and probably dead bodies probably litter the bottom.

"Poor people can be real jerks, too. Focus on people's strong points instead of criticizing their weak ones. Maybe they're having a bad day? Maybe they are under a lot of stress?"

"What if they really are rotten to the core?"

"Then perhaps you shouldn't associate with them."

"Essentially, you're saying I need to practice positive thinking?"

I'm positive I'm going to lose my patience with this snag.

"Absolutely. The people who say that money is the root of all evil are usually those that don't have any. One reason they have difficulty attracting it is because of the negative energy towards it.

"You'll easily attract what you desire when your positive thoughts become dominant. As soon as you believe that riches can create joy, you break down the walls."

"I must rid myself of all the negative thinking about it? There actually are some truly bad sides to wealth."

"There are many side effects of wealth—stress, complexity, separation of your peers, but if you can't completely rid yourself of the negative, then outweigh them with the positive."

"What do you mean?" I worked my fishing pole to the left and right, trying to free it, but nothing worked.

"One way of creating positive associations towards it is by having a cause. Fill in the blank—money is good because…"

"Money is good because I receive it by bringing value to others, therefore, making their lives better."

"See—this can unlock the door that is preventing you from being wealthy."

"That simple?"

"Yup."

With another large tug, my fishing line became limp.

Dang.

ℬaby 𝒮tep #51

"Jimmy Z!" the lady behind the counter yelled as we walked in through the door.

"Blissful Bella!" he returned as she ran from behind the counter to give him a big hug. One of the benefits of being a truck driver, I suppose.

I have to admit that her large brown eyes make my heart flutter a little—or it possibly might be all this caffeine.

"You're barely in time. I was about to close up." She locked the front door and turned to walk back around the counter.

She was more than a decade older than me. Her long brown hair flowed down her back and with her olive skin—her entire head appeared as if a chocolate fountain came alive.

In fact, her shop, Bella's Chocolate Bliss, seemed as if they completely made it of the delicious brown substance. I would've licked the walls if I had not had common sense to stop me.

"I figured we would pop in so my associate, Bud, could try one of your free samplers."

"Is that so?" She smiled.

"Well, I was sort of hoping to get one, too."

"I think you've had enough of my samplers."

She pulled two small trays with pink decorative paper out of the cupboard and set them on the counter in front of us. She then took some chocolates out of the display rack and placed five of them, evenly spaced, on each of our trays.

"Much appreciated."

"Yeah—thanks," I added.

They had various shapes and designs. I secretly hoped that they were all caramel, but I guess that would ruin the fun of it.

The eating area of the shop was large enough for three tables that seated two people each. Blissful Bella had to drag a chair from one of the other tables so she could join us.

"Bud, before eating each of those, I need you to think of a business you would be interested in launching. Then I would like you to yell, *'yes! I would like to start a...!'*"

"Nobody here but us, darling," she said as I looked over at her for approval.

"Yes! I want to start a motorcycle shop!" I yelled that with authority, though I did not toss the whole nugget in my mouth.

Oh, that's the devil's game there. No—any reasonable human knows they must bite it in half to be sure the other half is worth eating.

"Number fifty-one!"

"Fifty-one!" I shouted with strawberry nougat stuck to my teeth.

"When you first start out on your own, it'll be exciting, stressful, joyful, painful—everything all at once. There will be long, hard hours, exciting victories, and an emotional roller coaster that is addicting.

"When you glance back on your life, it'll probably be these first years that you are most fond of. Painful? Challenging? Rewarding? Absolutely."

"Yes! I want to start a dry cleaner!" I picked my second one and bit into it.

Pecans—gross!

"From about year three to about year seven, things are typically pretty fulfilling. There are still a lot of struggles and sometimes not enough profit to make it through the next month, but it's most definitely more stable. Plus, by this time, you'll have developed a routine and possibly won't need to work as much."

"Yes! I would like to start a restaurant!"

Dang—raspberry.

"Typically, from years seven to ten, it feels more like a job. It's not that you hate it, it's merely not as fun as it used to be. Nothing sparkles anymore.

"Your staff, if you have one, will seem like employees and not close friends, especially not the original ones you hired—the ones you still go to lunch with even though they've not been employed by you for years."

"Yes! I would like to start a used car dealership!"

Christmas mint... Acceptable.

"It'll almost become painful after ten years, though, but too good to give up. Business loans are low, profits are high, and it is a cash machine.

"It's at this point that you may want to hire a manager and step away from the daily operations, although you might try to tough it out and let it continue to drain your soul."

"This isn't always true. I started this shop right out of high school and I still love what I do."

"And I still love driving, so there are exceptions, of course."

"Yes! I want to start a chocolate shop."

Eureka! Caramel!

"Really?" She seemed surprised.

"You inspired me."

"Aaah…" She blushed.

My heart flickered.

"The average person usually operates for around ten years before they sell it or close up shop. If each of these were your businesses, then by the time you ate the first chocolate, you were thirty years old.

"The second one you were forty. The third, fifty. The fourth, sixty. As you bit into the fifth chocolate, you retired. As you finished it, you became just years away from the average lifespan of a man."

"Wow."

"To make matters worse, during the parts of your life that you own it, time will fly faster than you ever experienced before. You'll literally blink and be ten years older.

"You'll look back and remember doing all these things, but still can't figure out where the time went. This is what I meant earlier when I mentioned the depth of understanding—you are literally trading your life for your business."

"I…" I slumped over my empty tray.

"Here —" he said as he put one of his chocolates over on my tray. "I just gave you ten more years. Now knowing the true depth of what it is—what enterprise is worth that sacrifice?"

"I don't know." Instead of tossing it in my mouth, I sat there frozen.

"That is the toughest question that can be asked. That is why many don't answer it and settle for a much worse fate—by default, trading the same amount of life working for someone else, punching that time clock from nine to five."

"What do I do then?"

"Stop and take some time before you launch anything. You only get to say, *yes! I want to start this business!* so many times in your life before you're no longer able to ask it.

"Of all the things that you'll learn in entrepreneurship and in life—the answer to this question is all you need to know in order to win the game."

Chapter

Eighteen

Baby Step #52

"This mountain is relentless." I gasped for air. "Four hours of hiking and not a single level spot."

"Nope, and the rest of the trail is the same way."

He sat on the wood bench graciously provided by the forest service. He was barely breaking a sweat, one... Because he was used to hiking, and two... His backpack merely contained our sleeping bags.

My pack, weighing over forty pounds, had a metal frame and a strap that went around my waist to take the weight off of my back. Regardless, I bore all forty some odd pounds in my legs.

It carried everything other than the sleeping bags—the tent, a camping stove, pans, and whatever else we needed to camp overnight. What all was in there, I wasn't sure. He did the loading. I'm just the pack mule.

When I took it off and set it on the ground, I noticed the chill of the air touching the backside of my sweat-soaked shirt.

"Quite the view, isn't it?" I pulled my water and a granola bar out of the side pouch and I joined him on the bench.

I used the word *quite* intentionally. The Salt Lake valley had a lot of pollution and it made it hard to say it was beautiful.

"It's about to disappear from our view as soon as we cross over that ridge."

"How much longer before we hit the top?"

"We won't reach the peak until the morning. I'm planning to set up camp right below it. There's a large flat area I think you'll enjoy."

"Okay, then. How much longer before we reach our camp-site?" I chugged the better portion of my water bottle in what could be mistaken as one massive gulp.

"I'd say five to seven hours—depending on how much coughing and wheezing is going on behind me."

"Seven hours!"

"It all comes down to how you look at it. If you thought you had to hike at this incline for seven days, but then found out it was only seven hours—wouldn't it seem a lot smaller?"

"I guess so."

Perhaps I can trick myself into feeling like there is more granola bar to eat if I nibble at it.

"But what if I said it was really seven days? Would you be mentally prepared for that?"

"Not really."

"What if I said it took a month? After all, there are many summits on this planet that take longer to climb."

"That would be miserable."

"What if I said a year? One entire year of packing that gear up hill, all day every day, without rest?"

"I am not sure I could do it." I looked down and my granola wrapper was empty.

What happened? Did I really eat it that fast?

"Then how would you feel if it was ten years? A decade of your life span fighting to merely endure one more day, one more step? A decade where you are too busy to detect the passing of the years? A decade of your youth, gone?"

"That would be horrible."

"What if this was your entire existence? You graduate college and start climbing higher and higher. Next thing you know, you're retiring and all you know is this mountain. Not only your youth is gone but also all of your good years. And for what gain? What was the reward?"

"This isn't about hiking, is it?"

"No, it's really about—number fifty-two!"

"Fifty-two!"

"We are not meant to spend our entire lives in the state of constant struggle that business requires. If that was our entire existence, in the end, we would most likely be empty. Entrepreneurship is not intended to be an eternal battle—it is a muscle to be exercised to gain what we desire—now or in the long run."

"But you said the average business cycle takes ten years or more?"

"It does, but it doesn't take fifty. You must live life in between—you must live life during. Make sure that there are large periods of time away from your work—whether it be weeklong trips to the Caribbean, winters off for extended road trips, or years between projects traveling the world or spending moments with loved ones."

"I'm confused. Isn't becoming wealthy the purpose of becoming an entrepreneur? How do you do that if you take off so much time?"

"What about for those who aspire to lead a simple life, like myself? Does enterprise have to be for the sole sake of becoming wealthy? What about simply creating financial freedom in the quickest way?"

"That's…" *I'm not sure how to finish that sentence.*

"Look at my world. I own a small house that I consider a home base, but not really someplace I'd like to stay for very long. I drive truck for nine months a year and when it snows, I travel south and relax on a beach somewhere with a taco in my hand. Do I need to be rich for that lifestyle?"

"I guess not."

I wonder what the chances are that there is a taco shack at the summit of the hill. If there is, I'm sure it is a mirage. So sad.

"I swear to you—I lead a more rewarding life than most. I am wealthy in the important stuff. Being an owner-operator of my own transportation company allows me to take the time off to live. There are many enterprises that allow you to take a break with little or no consequences, like mine."

"But don't you lose loads while you're gone?"

"I do, but whatever clients I lose, there are ten more waiting in line. It all depends on the type of trade you choose. If you can find something that is high in demand, then you may come and go like it's a swinging door. You should not live your life so your business can exist. Your business should exist so you can live your life."

"Well, then, I guess this mountain isn't going to climb itself."

I picked up my backpack and started strapping it on.

Baby Step #53

"Okay—now this is impressive," I said as I walked over and sat on a large log. I unclipped my backpack, letting it fall backwards onto the ground.

As we crossed over the ridge, there was a small valley with three large ponds surrounded by prairie grass and pine trees. It could've been a painting if there was only a little cabin with smoke coming out of the chimney.

Conveniently placed overlooking the ponds, the log seemed to have been put there on purpose, but it was too large for that to be the case.

"I remember when I first saw these ponds." He looked genuinely happy as he joined me on the log.

"Well, I suppose we should begin cooking our dinner and setting our tent up. I'll grab the camp stove." I drug the massive backpack over the log and to the front of me.

"Yep, nothing worse than setting up camp without light."

"What the? Why did you bring an electric can opener? There's no power up here," I asked as I lifted it out of the bag.

"That's not any ordinary opener—that is name brand and stainless steel. Real top-of-the-line there." He smiled as if he was proud.

"What? And this?" I pulled out a bowling trophy.

"I wanted to impress you with my achievements."

"Is that a foot massager?" I looked up at him.

"I work hard and have earned the right to be comfortable." His tone suddenly turned defensive.

"Where's the food? Where's the camp stove? The tent is nowhere to be found!" My stomach grumbled as if it demanded to know the answer, too.

"That's ridiculous. There wasn't room for that stuff."

"We had room for all your stupid junk?"

"Junk? I thought we were friends, and I hoped to dazzle you with my shiny objects and achievements. I wanted you to accept me for who I am. And as for the foot massager, that's a standard of living that I insist on. You've no right to tell me I deserve less."

"But we are friends and I do accept you for who you are."

I mean this too—even if he dragged me up this stupid hill with no camp gear and, even worse, no taco shack at the top.

"You mean you accept me for being nothing more than a long-haired truck driver?"

"Of course—wait... Is this one of the Baby Steps?"

"We might as well get this out of the way—number fifty-three!"

"Really? We have to sleep in the dirt and go hungry because you decided to teach me something?"

I should hike down the mountain in the dark, but then again—I would prefer not to fist fight an angry badger.

"Sleeping in the dirt and being hungry is painful. I wanted to make good and sure that you remembered it because in the real world, this lesson *is* painful. In fact, it'll most definitely hold you back, destroy your dreams, and make your life an empty shell of what it could be."

"Fine—fifty-three!"

"There are two wrong phases during which to buy luxuries and creature comforts—the first is when you're starting out a business. Same as this backpack, there is only so much room in our present moment for complexity and materialism.

"For every useless shiny object that you needlessly cling onto, you may not have the room or the resources for something that you really need. I assure you that the massive house and the credit cards will hold you back."

"And the second?"

"The second is after you achieve success. The goal of achievements shouldn't be the acquisition of shiny objects and fancy cars."

"We can't own nice things until we become successful, and we can't own nice things afterwards either—then when should we acquire that stuff?"

"I'm not sure. When I come to that point, then I'll let you know."

"Then what is the point of working so hard?"

I assumed the answer was for shiny stuff and tacos. Possibly just tacos then?

"Of course, we must create value for others in order to survive—but do we need enterprise beyond that? How about instead of trading years of our treasured youth for shiny objects, the focus of our efforts should be for that of our freedom?"

"You keep mentioning freedom as if there's some magical force that controls us?"

"Money does. It is an essential part of living regardless of whether we like it. Though, a point we are able make is that if enterprise is a necessity of survival—then the more control we have over it, the less it can control us, the less time we need to labor over its attainment, the more freedom we get on how we live."

"As long as we're okay living without stuff?" I looked at the bowling trophy.

Perhaps it is chocolate wrapped in gold foil—like Christmas candy. I must be going delusional.

"The simple life does not have to be a poor one. However, financial freedom does not necessarily mean a wealthy one either. Simplicity truly means a daily presence low on complexity—not one with an empty checking account. In the same way, it doesn't take great wealth to enjoy freedom to lead a meaningful existence.

"When you're lying on the ground tonight wondering if a snake is going to crawl in your sleeping bag, ponder all the resources your business could be without because of needing irrelevant things."

"Snakes?" I jumped up and looked around at the ground.

"If one does crawl in with you—kill it so we may eat breakfast."

Baby Step #54

I plopped down on the dirt and hovered around the campfire for warmth, the Oracle sat on the only reasonably sized rock around. We rolled our campsite out, or should I say our sleeping bags without pillows, about fifty feet away over in the tall grass.

If I was a bear stumbling around in the dark and came across us lying there like human breakfast burritos, I'd be pretty happy.

"I see what you are talking about when you mention living a life of quality."

"It doesn't get much better than this."

"I can't believe that I have to head home after we hike down. This summer has sure gone by fast."

"You know you're welcome to ride along as long as you wish."

"I know, but I should return to my old life and prepare for my next phase. I appreciate all that you've done for me, though."

"Well, I enjoyed the company."

"It'll be strange to return to normal everyday life after this journey." Even though the front part of my body was being singed by the heat, the cool air nipped at the back of my neck.

"Speaking of returning to the real world, have you settled on what your first venture is going to be?"

"I'm leaning towards sticking with the motorcycle shop. It will be fairly simple to start. It's a great experience to cut my teeth on, and it'll allow me the winters off to travel and search within myself for what the next great *yes!* is to be."

"And that is your answer to the lofty question—what am I willing to trade this part of my youth for?"

"I think so. I mean, I don't want my entire existence to revolve around it, but I think it'll put me in a suitable position for what comes next."

"Very well then—number fifty-four!"

"Fifty-four!"

"After you've found a way to create value to others, written out in an exceptionally detailed and clear goal, researched your demographics, visited as many shops as possible, as to make it part of your reality—the next step is to bundle it up into a final vision and daydream about it as often as feasible."

"Daydream about it?"

That doesn't seem awfully productive.

"By trying to visualize it every moment you get, you construct the details and allow your mind to lock onto it—same as how a mountain lion will lock onto your face if he notices you tonight."

"Mountain lions? I was already worried about snakes and bears!" I quickly stood up and turned around, merely to see a darkness only found in nature.

"At least you don't need to worry about sharks."

"You're always the optimist."

The Golden Step

"And here you have it, Mount Sullivan!" The Oracle was way too enthusiastic for this hour of the morning.

We had already been hiking for almost an hour and a half or so and though the outline of the ridge was becoming prominent, we still needed our flashlights.

"Nice…" Between my attitude and my stomach, there was a lot of grumbling going on.

It didn't really matter when we left this morning—it wasn't as if I slept. I had visions of an oversized, fuzzy mountain monster clinging onto my face whenever I closed my eyes.

"Coffee?" He sat the King down on a rock ledge that was conveniently about waist high and twisted his cup off from the top. We were not quite at the peak, but this spot afforded us many places to sit and observe the sun coming up.

"Yep." I dug through the backpack of useless items, looking for anything I could use as a mug. However, the requirement of what was considered acceptable was pretty low, since he did not pack a camp stove and the coffee was the cold leftover stuff he made yesterday. I found my empty plastic water bottle and handed it to him. "Just half a bottle, please."

"That's good—that's about how much is left," he said after he filled his thermos cup.

I sat on the edge of the ledge observing the sky getting brighter with every minute as he carefully started pouring the bottom sludge into my container. My flashlight accented the rogue grounds that made it past the filter. Any other day I might not have drunk it.

What will this moment become to me in my memories? Or, for that fact, this entire summer? Will it be a thing that I pass off as a fun summer spent traveling? Will it become that same old story I tell my kids over and over? Will it define who I am to become?

What about the Oracle? Will we ever hang out again? Possibly grab lunch as he's passing through town someday? Or perhaps more? Maybe our paths might cross in our winter travels? I would like to say that he has become more than merely a teacher, or as in this day in particular, the guru who sits on top of the hill.

"There's one last lesson."

"The Golden Step?" I suddenly kicked the morning slumps out of my being as something brighter rushed in.

"Are you ready to receive its message?"

"I believe so."

My hand shook faintly, as if I had the java jitters. Though I hadn't taken a sip. Was it possible that his coffee was so strong that I could absorb the caffeine through my skin?

"Okay, then."

"Okay." I took a chug off my bottle of black sunshine as my face involuntarily twitched—this was most definitely caused by his atrocious trucker coffee.

"I'll need you to close your eyes for this because I'll have you visualize some things."

"And miss the best part of the sunrise?"

"This'll only take a minute."

When I slid back on the rock ledge, I could lift my legs and cross them in front of me. I set my black sunshine down, put my hands on my knees to brace myself, and shut my eyes. "Okay, I'm ready."

"I ask that you take a deep breath in and relax." He took a deep breath in, too. "I'll speak slowly, so your mind has a chance to visualize this."

"That's fine."

"Imagine that, after decades on earth, you are now approaching the pearly gates. There are puffs of clouds everywhere and a large, shiny gold gate. All that is remaining now is who you have become.

"Who are you? Do you like who you've developed into? Are you at peace with spending eternity as this person? What did you leave behind? Did you leave the world a better place? Other than your family, will people still remember you in fifty years? Ten years? How about tomorrow?

"As you walk closer to the gate, you spot a gigantic television screen that is replaying you a single day that you lived. Suddenly, beams of light shoot out of the television and draw you in, allowing you not only to observe this day over again, but you experience it with all of your senses. You experience the emotions you had, but you're unable to change them now. You must play it out the same way as it was.

"Being able to reflect on that day, knowing this may be the last opportunity you get to see it, how do you feel? Did you make the most of your time, or do you feel regret? Do you wish you had paid more attention to your surroundings? Maybe paid more attention to the people that are no longer around?

"How about the long hours you spent at work or growing your business? Do you wish you had done more during the moments when you didn't work? Did you devote too much energy to tasks that you now consider pointless? What are some things you wasted time on?

"To get past the pearly gates, now imagine that you are the sole person who has to judge your days on earth. You were only given five days that were randomly chosen to experience again. How would these five days appear to you? If you used them as the average sum of your life, how would you feel about it?

"If you spent three out of the five days solely going through the motions, going to work and then watching six hours of television, how would you feel about that? Take these days into account as the entirety of your life. Do you believe you are deserving of crossing the gates into whatever lies beyond?

"Now imagine that it trapped you inside this television and you spend all of eternity reliving every second of every day. Would you consider your life meaningful? Would you enjoy it or would it torture you? Would you be happy with the way things turned out?

"Perhaps you would wish that you had done things differently? That you had been more active with your free moments? You had spent more time enjoying these years? You had given more to others? You had built better relationships?

"What if heaven and hell were just reliving every second of your former days over and over and how you spent them would determine whether or not you considered it heaven? Open your eyes."

"That was intense."

Rays of sunlight were spreading throughout the sky as if the sun was stretching its arms, yawning, and preparing for a new day.

"The good news is that you're not dead yet and you still have an opportunity to change things into the way you would like them to be.

"You want to contribute more to others? Don't forget to be remembered. Spreading joy is a good start. You want a better job? Take action about it now rather than being regretful about it later. Do you want better relationships with others? Then make an effort to be with them. Do you want to enjoy each day more? Do that by taking time to stop and look around."

"I guess what follows in my story is a blank page. But how do I build this better life when the fact is that I must trade some of it for funds in order for survival?"

"You're right. The unfortunate side of society today is that it's virtually essential to earn money to survive. You may have to spend some of your precious youth to create value for someone else. Not many people can bring in an income from fishing.

"So, the question is—how do you do this? How do you work without having regret when you consider the duration that you spend doing it?"

"I don't know how to answer that." I looked over at him.

"First, the less you spend and the more intelligent you are with your money, the less you need the money. That means that you spend less of your days earning it and more camping with your family."

"A life without excessive complexity and useless materialism? Sign me up."

Who am I? I would've never uttered those words three months ago.

"Second, since you'll still need some cold hard cash regardless of your spending habits, it boils down to finding something that you love to do and brings value to others. You need to find an endeavor that if you were to look back at the period you spent working at it for the rest of eternity, you would still feel passionate about it.

"Do you think Michelangelo regrets the days that he spent creating sculptures or painting great works of art for others to enjoy? Do you think Abraham Lincoln regrets fighting for justice in America? Do you think I'm likely to have any regrets? I could, but I'm going to do everything in my power while I am here to not have any."

"Is this what the Baby Steps are about?" The sunrise developed a bright yellow halo as the skies turned blue.

"Yes, the simple theories of them are—find something you love and do it. Don't let others tell you that you can't, because you can. Make more time for the people you care for and don't allow them to drift away. Steer clear of letting possessions such as boats and flashy cars stand in your way—let go of what is needed in order to make the overall quality of your life more desirable.

"If at the end of your days—this combined accumulation of moments are all that you take with you—then there's not a single one you can afford to waste."

"Thank you."

"Always remember this—it is not the pursuit of money. It is the pursuit of happiness."

The Oracle's Golden Step is a part of the
Brian's Seed of Truth series. For more information on this
topic or ones similar to it, please follow us at:

briansseedoftruth.com

<u>Youtube</u>
Brian's Seed of Truth
@briansseedoftruth6282

<u>Tik Tok</u>
@briansseedoftruth

<u>Instagram</u>
briansseedoftruth

<u>Twitter</u>
Brian's Seed of Truth
@B_SeedOfTruth

www.ingramcontent.com/pod-product-compliance
Lightning Source LLC
Chambersburg PA
CBHW030456210326
41597CB00013B/691